Reflections of a Former Atheist

by Glen Doss

Reflections of a Former Atheist
Glen Doss
2012 Frontier Press

Doss, Glen
Reflections of a Former Atheist

September 2012

frontier press
THE SALVATION ARMY USA WESTERN TERRITORY

DEDICATION

Dedicated to the glory of God and with appreciation to my partner-in-Christ, my wife Mary, who has supported me through so much growth, and also to my children, Chris and Jennifer, whom I love with all my heart.

I also wish to express my immense gratitude to The Salvation Army, which has provided me with so many opportunities to reach out in love to hurting people in the name of Christ. I continue to be overwhelmed by the joy that comes through service.

When we have become sensitive to the painful contours of our hostility we can start identifying the lines of its opposite toward which we are called to move: hospitality.

— Henri J. M. Nouwen
Reaching Out: The Three Movements of the Spiritual Life

TABLE OF CONTENTS

PREFACE

This volume chronicles the development of my personal outlook on life. It recounts the results of mistaken beliefs and relates my spiritual rebirth. The story is presented from the perspective of important moments of my life, each followed by a reflection from my current viewpoint as a Christian. My hope is that God is glorified through this story and readers will be blessed.

DISCLAIMER

While all the accounts recorded in this manuscript did occur, with few exceptions the names (and nicknames) of the people have been changed to preserve anonymity. Those that have not been altered are as follows:

Chapter 4	Daddy Willis (my grandfather on my mother's side)
Chapter 11	Chris and Jennifer, my son and daughter Herb Scott, former European *Stars & Stripes* city editor
Chapter 17	My brother, Dale Doss, a Freewill Baptist minister
Chapters 19–20	John and Ann Nute, San Diego Citadel Corps local officers
Chapter 21	Margaret Foster, San Diego Citadel Corps member
Chapters 24–26	My wife, Mary

PART I
FORMATIVE YEARS

CHAPTER ONE

Blessed are the Pure in Heart

WHEN I WAS A CHILD, there was a patch of woods behind our southern Arkansas farm that I used as my own private sanctuary. I would go there to meet with God. A shady nook some 12 by 20 feet in size, it was hemmed in by pines intertwined with blackberry bushes and brambles. Leaves served as my carpet, while a slash of light from the sky above doubled as my chandelier. Because it was only accessible by a crawlspace so small that an adult could not enter it, I was certain that no other human being had ever trespassed there.

Seeking privacy from the intimidating world about me, I found reclusion in this sanctum whenever I could. And it was there I told my private prayers to God. In this haven, which seemed so secretive and safe, I was alone with him. He was my friend, my invisible, tender friend. Something of a loner, I mixed little with other children, but God was always welcome for company.

Despite the threatening tones of our preacher's sermons, somewhere along the way I came to see God as a caring confidant. In my grassy hideaway, I shared with him my special secrets and listened as he called me his very own. To this treasured refuge I spirited my books: Grimm brothers' fairy tales and adventures by Jack London. With God as my companion, I had a reading buddy, one who wouldn't chastise me when I made a mistake, but was forgiving of my foibles and thrilled along with me as the knight rescued the damsel from the dreaded dragon's lair.

From the lips of children and infants
you have ordained praise … (Ps. 8:2 NIV)

A sharp cry of glee catches the world off guard
as vigilant deer jerk their heads up high
and perk up their ears, then knowingly sigh,
"A small boy is at hand—God's own is nearby!"

The child glides over the meadows.
He slides through the shadows,
takes the sunlight for a spin.
He frolics with the angels and then
impulsively pauses beside a rose garden,
free spirit aflame with the splendor of God,
excited, delighted by the grandeur of God!

Near cool, baptismal streams he dallies
when comes a clarion call,
"I am a rose of Sharon, a lily of the valleys,"
down the mind's own canyons,
through the hollows of the soul!

Virtually a virgin to the wide world's ways,
the child falls yearning to his knees,
then peers and pores over
dew-sparkling spider webs—delicately laced,
mysteriously suspended, in the breeze trembling—
eyes wide with awe, a pure, wondering gaze.

At the mountainside of Time, the young child stands,
terrifyingly small against a measureless span
that meteorically sprawls
from vast canyon to canyon, wide wall to wall,
long straining to stare through that numinous glare
at the elusive future awaiting him there.
Despite the broad barrier, the child doggedly squints
through bright, blinding sunlight, long searching for hints,
till, piqued at the utter futility,
he turns with a forced servility.

The inquisitive but spirited,
impassioned, innocent child
remains eerily unaware
how all listening nature reverently bows
as the angels say their fervent prayers:

"Lord, as he moves to meet his future,
protect him, guard him from himself
and all fiendish evil conspiring there."

BIBLE SELECTION

[T]he disciples came to Jesus with the question, "Who is really greatest in the kingdom of Heaven?" Jesus called a little child to his side and set him on his feet in the middle of them all. "Believe me," he said, "unless you change your whole outlook and become like little children you will never enter the kingdom of Heaven. It is the man who can be as humble as this little child who is greatest in the kingdom of Heaven.... Be careful that you never despise a single one of these little ones—for I tell you that they have angels who see my Father's face continually in Heaven (Matt. 18:1-4, 10 Phillips).

REFLECTION

In retrospect it is a marvel to me how close a relationship I had with God when I was very young. At the time it seemed entirely unexceptional—it was just the way things were. God was there; I was there; we relished each other's company. Today I know the reason this early relationship existed is because a personal relationship with God is the most natural thing in the world. A small child is nothing if not natural. A small child cannot put on a pretense.

The Quaker college professor Rufus Jones recognized this:

> I am convinced by my own life and by wide observation of children that mystical [spiritual] experience is much more common than is usually supposed. Children are not so absorbed as we are with things and with problems. They are not so completely organized for dealing with the outside world as we older persons are. They do not live by cut-and-dried theories. They have more room for surprise and wonder. They are more sensitive to intimations, flashes, openings. The invisible impinges on their souls and they feel its reality as something quite natural.[1]

Dear Lord, I recall my submissive spirit as a child—the way I trustingly looked up to you and talked with you. When, years later, in the face of increasingly insurmountable difficulties, I finally relinquished my heavy burden of self-adoration and turned to you once more with the trusting spirit of a child, you unhesitatingly welcomed me back home! Like the father in Christ's parable who, upon seeing his lost son returning, was filled with compassion, you too with great joy took me into your arms and held me close—as you have consistently been doing ever since. Thank you, Lord, for loving me despite my many grave errors, mistakes that caused hurt to so many down through the years.

In the precious name of Jesus Christ my Savior I pray. Amen.

CHAPTER TWO

The Beginnings of Dissonance

WILLIE AND HENRIETTA BROWN lived alone in a clapboard house a half mile down the road from us when I was a kid. Perched high up in an oak in our front yard, I would often see Willie working long hours in his garden. As he raked and hoed, the rhythmical rocking of those broad shoulders spoke to me of patience and a large soul. Willie always had a kind word for a boy like me. And in a special way, I loved him.

As the oldest child, by age five I was permitted to trail after my dad as he did the morning chores. I raced behind him, traipsing across the field or going around by the dirt road that led from our house to the Browns'. While we certainly weren't well off, our home compared ostentatiously with the Browns' three-room hovel—the front porch had gaping holes and the window screens were corroded and torn. The Browns, who were black, were in their 50s. My parents' relationship with them framed the way I, a white child, would view African-Americans for many years to come.

My eyes as round as moons, my ears alert to every nuance, I looked on intrigued as Daddy knocked at their front door. Their eyes never failed to brighten nor their voices to emanate cheer as Daddy explained the reason for his call, which was often to ask Willie to do some chore for pay. Daddy usually brought a gift for them: chicken eggs from our hen house or vegetables from our garden. Regardless of what it was, Willie and Henrietta always gleefully accepted.

Despite the evident condescension, I believe Daddy felt sincere affection for the Browns. I'm sure he truly liked and respected every person in our rural community, regardless of their race or status. But since then I have often wondered if his fondness for the Browns was reciprocated, or was their well-honed civility simply sycophancy and no more.

Willie and Henrietta often knocked on our front door or tapped upon the screen, and I would gaily run to greet them. After all, they were our good friends, always ready with a joke and a laugh. However, although we often had white folks in for coffee or iced tea or to dine with us at mealtime, not so with Willie and Henrietta; my parents visited with them outside on the porch. When I asked why, I was informed: "It's because they're colored, son. Coloreds aren't permitted inside the house." This explanation was given frankly and in absolute sincerity, though the logic of it escaped me entirely.

In the view of much of the Southern white population (the only group for which I feel I can speak), dark-skinned people in the 1950s were considered lower class. And this perception was very, very real. No matter how bad off you were financially—even homeless and living beneath a bridge—if your skin was white you were considered of significantly higher status than a black man or woman with a fine home and money in the bank.

This discrepancy was evident as I noted the stark contrast between the condition of the public school I attended and that of the other attended by our black neighbors, just a half mile down the road. Peering curiously through a window one day, I was struck by its grossly dilapidated state— cracked windows and walls, and half-broken desks conspicuously carved with the names of long-gone students. The building was a simple wooden structure with peeling paint, while our "white school" consisted of a number of new brick buildings. Looking on one day as our school custodian carted several boxes of used textbooks into the back of a pickup truck, I queried, "Mr. Jenkins, what are you doing with all those old books?"

He explained matter-of-factly that he was taking them over to the school for black kids, adding, "We give them all the old stuff when our new supplies come in." And so I understood—they got our leftovers. They didn't merit new books.

Though quite puzzled by the contradiction inherent in the practice and custom handed down to me—black people were our friends, yet they were not our social equals—I accepted it as straightforwardly as I accepted all other things taught to me at the time. So it was that sometime early on in life, I ceased seeing Willie and Henrietta as just good friends and came to believe that, while they were nice people, they were somehow not as worthy as we white folks and therefore should be treated differently. In retrospect, I can see that my awareness of the contradiction never ceased plaguing me but continued to smolder at a shallow, albeit subliminal, level for many years to come.

* * *

As surely as I shiver while a winter wind howls outside my window today, I sense a winter storm blowing through the oaks of yesteryear. I am six years old. A breezy, chilly night—midnight. Billowing clouds appear ominous as lightning streaks the sky and thunder rolls with a sound like that of a bowling ball violently striking pins. I burrow beneath my covers, pulling them tightly to my chin.

The Browns' house trembles against the ferocity of the storm. A fork of lightning slashes the darkness; my eyes pop open. Glancing out the window, I glimpse a midnight world in daytime colors. Two hunched figures race against the storm, their coats clasped tightly at the neck. Over the rush of the rain, I hear kicked pebbles striking stones and the murmur of muffled voices. A screen door bangs. A man's voice calls. I hear my parents moving through the hall.

"It's Willie and Henrietta," Mama whispers. "Why! They're soaking wet!" Minutes later: "Honey, they want to know if they can wait out the storm with us. They're deathly afraid their house is going to be blown away!"

A long silence. I hold my breath.

"Of course," I hear Daddy murmur. "It's a bad one. Bring them in."

I lower myself from the bed. Barefoot, clad only in my underwear, I tiptoe to the door. Opening it as gently as I can, I peep around the corner. Sure enough, there are Willie and Henrietta sitting on our sofa, thanking my parents in hushed voices for providing a haven from the storm. And so it is that the taboo is broken—the one and only time I recall seeing black folks in our house. I am astonished at the incongruity of the scene—Willie and Henrietta in our living room, drinking coffee, having a civil conversation with my parents!

Mama and Daddy appear patronizing, very uncomfortable in the face of the bizarre situation. After a few minutes, I tiptoe back to my bed as my mother returns to hers. For a long while I hear only Daddy's voice drumming on, the murmur broken occasionally by nervous laughter from Willie and Henrietta. Eventually I drift off to sleep.

Rushing outdoors the following morning, I confront a wet, wind-blown world. Broken branches are perched in the oddest places. The creek running along our fields has overflowed its banks, dumping huge streams of water into ditches where fish and crawdads now abound. The sharp report of a swinging hammer slashes the air—Willie hard at work mending his house. I see Henrietta gathering up limbs and trash from their yard.

Me? I am reeling from the miracle of the night before, my head in a spin. An African-American couple, my old friends Willie and Henrietta, had visited in our home. I check out the sofa where they sat and marvel at the absence of any evidence. There is no change at all.

BIBLE SELECTION

Peter told them, "You know it is against the Jewish laws for me to come into a Gentile home like this. But God has shown me that I should never think of anyone as impure.... I see very clearly that God doesn't show partiality" (Acts 10:28, 34 NLT).

REFLECTION

I have been in many discussions on the subject of racial prejudice, particularly the double standard practiced for so many years in the southern United States, which in some form still lingers on. In discussing the pre-1965 era, when segregated schools, restaurants and public bathrooms were the norm, the observation is often made: Racial prejudice is such a vile thing. How could people be so bigoted? How could people have participated in such a conspiracy of cruelty?

Such prejudicial practices are almost without question considered cruel; yet one thing I detected then and today remember well is the tenderness and love evident in my father's demeanor and voice as he mingled with the poor African-Americans, our neighbors, whom he hired to do much of the work on the farm. He loved these people deeply and was acquainted personally with many of them. Yet though he loved them, he still treated them as second-class citizens—of somewhat less worth than the rest of us—not because he was cruel, but because this was the structure that defined the world he knew.

When Southern white people of that era looked out at the world, they didn't see the racial parameters—rather the parameters themselves were part and parcel of the lens through which they viewed their world. It was the way the world was, straight out, as far as they could see.

Dear Lord, I have learned that I am not capable of forming right judgments without your aid. Open my eyes to the truth and show me how to be an effective witness to others of your presence in my life. Break through the crust of biases implanted during my childhood. Send your divine light through me and reveal for me the truth.

In the precious name of Jesus Christ my Savior I pray. Amen.

CHAPTER THREE

A Memorable Lesson in Humility

IF THERE WAS ONE LESSON brought home to me more emphatically than any other when I was a child, it was the tremendous respect that we kids were taught to have for our elders—the older the person, the greater the deference. Therefore, when one day the males and females in our country church were separated—the women filing off to one room, the men to another (my father and I among them)—I was bewildered. At only six years old, I was unaccustomed to being included with the adults. There were only two or three of us small boys in the group of 15 or 20 males.

Agog, I watched as a man took a pan of water and a washcloth, then stooped and removed the shoes of another man and began systematically washing his feet. When he finished, he dried the feet with a towel. Then the two men reversed roles—the man whose feet had been washed now washed and dried the feet of the other. As the pan was passed along, I watched the others do likewise. I was mesmerized, having no clue as to what was going on. I was too young to grasp the teaching of the gospel account in John 13 of Christ washing his disciples' feet. I simply knew that these men were doing something astonishing.

Then the most wonderful thing of all occurred. A man in his 80s got slowly down upon his knees in front of me and peered directly into my face. With a twinkle in his eyes, he smiled. Sensing my confusion, he remarked pleasantly, "How are you, son?"

Wide-eyed and befuddled, I think I nodded—I don't recall for sure—but what I do remember is my amazement, for my world had been flipped upside down. The elderly gentleman, whom I held in the highest regard, gently removed my socks and shoes. "What are you doing?" I questioned.

"I'm going to wash your feet," he said, "like Jesus washed his disciples' feet, the way the preacher described."

"But why? Are they dirty?"

He grinned. "No. No. They're not dirty. It's just a custom we have. I'm washing your feet to show how much I care for you, just as Jesus washed his disciples' feet to show how much he cared for them and to show his humility. Likewise, we demonstrate our humility—one toward another."

"Oh," I said, though now I was more confused than ever. The elderly gentleman rubbed the dampened rag gingerly over my ankles and feet, took a towel and thoroughly dried them, then replaced my socks and shoes.

I felt a deep sense of wonder as I watched this extraordinary act. It was a complete reversal of our roles as I had come to understand them. I contemplated the marvel of this unusual experience for many years to come: one day an old man knelt to wash a little boy's feet.

BIBLE SELECTIONS

Jesus knew that his hour had come to leave this world and return to his Father. He now showed the disciples the full extent of his love.... So he got up from the table, took off his robe, wrapped a towel around his waist, and poured water into a basin. Then he began to wash the disciples' feet and to wipe them with the towel he had around him (John 13:1, 4-5 NLT).

"[W]hoever wants to become great among you must be your servant, and whoever wants to be first must be your slave—just as the Son of Man did not come to be served, but to serve, and give his life as a ransom for many" (Matt. 20:26-28 NIV).

REFLECTION

The awkwardness I felt when the elderly gentleman stooped to wash my feet accentuates the disparity between Jesus' teachings and the world's usual practices. Christ taught emphatically that many of the accepted customs of his day (and ours) are not approved by God and are not congruent with God's perspective. The world emphasizes: "Look out for number one!" while Christ teaches: *"[T]ake the lowest place"* (Luke 14:10 NIV).

Two decades ago, dear Lord, I gladly took your yoke upon myself with the full and willful determination to learn from you, and I consequently found your promised rest for my soul (Matt. 11:29). *"It is enough for the student to be like his teacher,"* you inform me, because *"a student is not above his teacher"* (Matt. 10:24-25 NIV); therefore, dear Lord, please grant me the perennial grace of humility. Help me to consistently honor others above myself (Rom. 12:10). May I remember every day how precious all people are in your eyes, how close to your heart each one is. Yours is a broken heart, dear Jesus; may mine be also. Keep me humble before the honor of your great sacrifice for me.

Today I kneel before you alongside the lowest of the low upon the earth—the woman who reeks of filth and alcohol, the child begging for a crumb, the man who has burned all his bridges, the murderer pleading for forgiveness, the impertinent youth who has *"come to his senses"* (Luke 15:17 NIV). All of these, dear God, I kneel alongside, for they are more precious to you than rubies or pearls. Thank you, dear Lord, for your purifying Spirit, your cleansing blood which knocks the pride full-force out of me and brings me low as I kiss your sweet feet. I praise you, Lord Jesus, because you have forgiven and forgotten all my gross transgressions in the purity of your perfect heart.

Today the child—who was long ago awed by the kind, humble gesture of an elderly farmer—has been broken and beaten by life, stung by Satan's lies, and come to you, dear Lord, to beg forgiveness. Finally lost in your warm embrace, sincerely I turn my life and will over to you.

In the precious name of Jesus Christ my Savior I pray. Amen.

CHAPTER FOUR

The Face of Death

I LOVED DADDY WILLIS with the affection only a trusting child can feel. My mother's father, he was a precious wave of warm love washing over my early childhood. He flooded into my life and out again before I was old enough to know him; I was just seven at his passing. But two clear memories, two gems, stand out starkly in my mind.

One was of a shiny red rocker, just my size, a miniature he built for me when I was five. I recall him presenting the gift to me, waving to me to come try it out, and, when I did, his face lighting up like a Christmas tree. Rocking back and forth with all the gusto I could muster, enjoying my new treasure, that was my gift to him. My mother oohed and ahhed as if the present were another baby. Crafted by his own calloused hands, the rocker remained at my parents' house for decades. Whenever I saw it, I thought of him, the man I loved before I knew what love was, whose memory remains so dear to me.

The other recollection is of Cracker Jacks®, that tasty confection of glazed popcorn and peanuts that every American child of the '50s enjoyed. It was my grandfather's practice whenever he went downtown to Hamburg, the county seat six miles away, to bring a package back for me. One instance stands out strongly in my mind, perhaps because he passed soon after, for the memory came rushing back as I peered into his casket. I remember him turning his old gray pickup off the muddy gravel road, steering it between the tall oaks shading our front lawn. Slowing to a crawl, he shouted to get my attention where I was at play in the yard: "Hey, boy! Hey, son! Look what I brought cha!"

Recognizing his voice, I came running, gleeful and excited. "Daddy Willis! Daddy Willis! Have you got more Cracker Jacks for me?"

"Of course! How could I ever forget you?" From the cab window, he flung the familiar box with the blue sailor boy on the cover over the fence into our front yard, then, laughing, he slowly drove away, looking back at me over his shoulder. Me? I was lost in the sweet concoction of glazed popcorn and peanuts. It was a seemingly trivial incident, but the memory of that exchange became one of the treasured highlights of my young childhood.

Shortly afterward, I witnessed another scene which was to make sense only in its aftermath—the image of my beautiful, young mother standing beneath the oaks bordering our lawn, her whole body racked with sobs; she was just 27 years old at the time. Terrified and deeply confused, I watched helplessly from our front porch as she held her head in her hands and screamed at the top of her lungs. Transfixed, I stared at her, begging her to stop. Yet I could not get her attention; her heart was far, far away, lost in waters too deep for such a small child to tread. I found I couldn't rescue her from such great depths. I could not understand what was happening, for what can a seven-year-old grasp of such deep grief?

A few days later, friends and relatives gathered in the small weather-beaten house where my grandparents lived, less than a mile from our own. Daffodils were in bloom. Hummingbirds made their rounds, their wings fluttering rapidly in the air, hovering over the bright yellow harbingers of spring.

I followed my parents into the house to join a crowd milling about, coffee cups in hand, murmuring in low and somber tones. Uncomprehending and feeling out of place, I was glad when the adults ushered us kids outdoors. There were several kids my age and I was thrilled. "Let's play cowboys and Indians!" suggested Ronnie. Using our hands as six-guns, we chased each other around the field, hollering out: "Bang! Bang! Bang!"

"I shot you; you're dead!" called out Carl. Grabbing my chest, I tumbled into the tall grass and lay still, attempting to appear as deathlike as possible, not having a clue what death was about.

Soon our mothers appeared at the door, dabbing their eyes with their handkerchiefs. "Boys, come on in. It's time for the viewing," my aunt called, her voice broken. It was then that I realized there was something dire and different about this family gathering.

We hadn't the slightest idea what my aunt meant. "The viewing? What's that?" I asked. My cousins didn't know either. Then in the living room a bizarre sight caught my attention. A procession of people formed a broken circle that commenced at the front door and wrapped around the furniture, terminating at a large ornamented wooden box where the visitors paused and glanced down. Some burst into sobs and clutched the box with agitated hands. Others, after a single furtive glance, turned their eyes embarrassingly away. I could not for the life of me fathom what was going on.

My parents nudged me along with them in the little procession. As we drew nearer, my mother began to cry again, the tears growing more profuse the closer we came to the front of the line, and I realized that her sadness was somehow linked to the large box. I found myself in a confused state of ambivalence—strangely attracted, yet at the same time repelled by the mysterious wooden object.

Finally I caught a glimpse of my grandfather's face, and my heart seemed to skip a beat. I gasped! "It's Daddy Willis—it's him! What's going on?" I remarked, startled, glancing up at my parents.

"He's dead, son," whispered my father. My mother's hand tightened on mine, a sob escaping her. I still did not understand; I hadn't a clue. Standing on tiptoe, I saw his face more clearly, my head just a little higher than the top of the casket. My grandfather's eyes were closed, his mouth prim, the face muscles relaxed, and his cheeks appeared tinted an exaggerated red. His whole body was lain out and I noted he was wearing his church suit. He seemed in a deep, deep sleep.

Then it hit me that he was dead—dead in the way that animals die, for this kind of death was familiar to me. I knew that upon their death they ceased to move and eventually their bodies decayed. I had seen snakes torn apart by the sharp blades of the pasture mower. Once I had run toward the fierce barking of dogs that had cornered a cat, and stood by helpless and horrified as they tore the poor screaming animal to bits. On another occasion I had watched intently as my dad drew a bead on a hog, hoping to hit it squarely between the eyes so its death would come quickly. When the aim proved untrue, I observed with dismay my father's open grief as the animal, howling, died a slow and painful death.

But until now, all the people I had seen were alive and vital, moving, active, their eyes aglow and their limbs strong. Standing by the coffin, in awe I studied the immobile form. He certainly resembled Daddy Willis, but was missing the twinkle in the eyes and the vivacious, rolling laughter I had come to associate with him. This seemed some stranger, some imposter, and I could not accept that it really was my grandfather. I gazed down at the body, trying to take it all in, but the longer I looked, the more confused I became.

When we finally moved on, my father trying to comfort my mother, I wandered away, out of doors, onto the grass, pondering the mysteries of life and death as only a small child can. On that day a seed was planted that was to evolve eventually into the soulless, mechanistic philosophy that by age 13 was to define my worldview.

For if humans die in the same way as birds and cats and cattle, are we not all made of the same stuff? If our deaths are so similar, what of our births? For I had seen a calf emerge from its mother's womb, enwrapped in placenta. I had watched in fascination as a mother cat gave birth to kittens, then begin weakly, persistently licking the newborns clean. If animals were born and died in similar ways, what about procreation? Here, too, I was to learn that humans had much in common with animals. I had seen a rooster grip the feathers on the back of a hen's head with his beak and copulate shamelessly in the open. For what does a brute animal know of shame?

There were hard roads yet to be traveled before I would understand something of the grace of God. As the years went by, I became increasingly insistent that I must be able to get my head around a concept before I would accept it—even the concept of whether there is a God. Uncomprehending God's plan, I was doomed to go through much misery before I would find peace; one day, years later, I would fall humbly to my knees and admit: I cannot begin to understand all the reasons why things are the way they are, but because I KNOW there is a God in the world, no matter how wrong things seem to be, they are still alright. Things are alright with God and his world.

BIBLE SELECTIONS

We know that the same God who raised our Lord Jesus will also raise us with Jesus and present us to himself.... Though our bodies are dying, our spirits are being renewed every day. For our present troubles are quite small and won't last very long. Yet they produce for us an immeasurably great glory that will last forever! (2 Cor. 4:14, 16-17 NLT).

The last enemy to be destroyed is death.... "Where, O death, is your victory? Where, O death, is your sting?" (1 Cor. 15:26, 55 NIV).

REFLECTION

As I peered down into the coffin at my grandfather's quiet and kindly face, yet with the mortician's makeup so clownish in appearance, a chill rippled up and down my spine. Something exploded within me that continued to reverberate 14 years later as I carried my buddies' broken bodies in Vietnam. The teaching in our community church never hit home; the notion of eternal life in Christ never quite sank in. My only thought was that death was the annihilation of one's life. And who wants his life to come to an end?

"The idea of death, the fear of it, haunts the human animal like nothing else," observed psychologist Ernest Becker in his Pulitzer Prize-winning book *The Denial of Death*.[2] Becker is on to something inasmuch as he speaks for the atheist; however, his statement does not ring true for one living in God.

I once was the former, haunted by the deaths of my comrades in war, driven mad by the apparent senselessness of living, dreading and fearing my own demise. Yet, later, still an atheist, I longed for death, which I had come to view as merely the cessation of existence and, hence, the end of the painful emotional and spiritual trauma that beset me. I saw death as a relief, simply falling off into a deep and peaceful sleep, the kind from which you don't wish to be aroused when the bedside alarm goes off and, groaning, you reach for the snooze button. *Who would not want that?* I asked myself, when life as I knew it was one long, torturous experience.

After I was saved, I viewed death in a whole new light, knowing that after the demise of the body, a loving God remains with his child, who continues to live on, no longer encumbered by the broken frame lying outstretched in the grave. I became aware that the God who works the miracle of generating life inside the mother's womb also brings about eternal life for the one who loves him; he who works the first miracle can certainly accomplish the second.

Basking today in the joy of the Lord, I move between the world of the living and the dead with ease, from the dedication of an infant to a graveside funeral service, experiencing no lessening of the joy of the Lord. God embraces both; the second is as natural as the first, for there is no death for those who have received the gift of his joy, his perennial, all-fulfilling joy.

Dear Lord, thank you for your priceless gift of eternal life. I pray that we will never take this precious gift for granted, that we will not—via osmosis from the secular world all about us—come to adopt a cold, sterile, mistaken notion of death, so different from the account given in Scripture. For you, the Creator, made us for more than this world. The proof, if we dare look for it, is written within our own hearts where we know intuitively that we are linked with the divine (Eccl. 3:11; John 1:9). Humbly we kneel and honor you and accept your precious gift of everlasting life.

In the precious name of Jesus Christ my Savior I pray. Amen.

CHAPTER FIVE

The Lure of God's Spirit

AT AGE SEVEN I WAS mesmerized by our minister. Still today I can see him bellowing out hallelujahs as enormous globules of sweat drip from his forehead and nose. He doesn't miss a beat as a huge hand disappears inside a shirt pocket, retrieving a bandanna with which he distractedly wipes his face. To my young mind, his sermon is flawless; he is a superhero, his message beyond all doubt hitting home. He paces the aisle like a hungry leopard on the prowl, challenging each man, woman and child as they sit clapping, tapping and singing in the little congregation. He flings, it appears, not only his words but his whole being at each member of the excited flock. "Don't you feel the Holy Ghost, brothers and sisters? God pleads with you: 'Come!' So come this evening! Kneel before him. The Ancient of Days sees into your hearts. He knows! He knows!"

Pointing up to the ceiling, squinting dark and piercing eyes, he shouts, "As the stones struck him and he felt his life ebbing away, the martyr Stephen announced, *'Behold, I see the heavens opened and the Son of Man standing on the right hand of God'* [Acts 7:56 KJV].

"Christ lives, ladies and gentlemen, and he will come again soon. As their beloved Lord rose to the heavens before their very eyes, his disciples watched till he was lost from sight, amazed but forlorn, aggrieved, feeling lost and abandoned, until the angels appeared and stunned them with the announcement: *'Ye men of Galilee, why stand ye gazing up into heaven? This same Jesus, which is taken up from you into heaven, shall so come in like manner as ye have seen him go into heaven!'* [Acts 1:11 KJV].

"The apostle Paul assures us: *For the Lord himself shall descend from heaven with a shout, with the voice of the archangel, and with the trump of God, and the dead in Christ shall rise first. Then we which are alive and remain shall be caught up together with them in the clouds, to meet the Lord in the air* [1 Thess. 4:16-17 KJV].

"The Lord's word to us, brothers and sisters, is that we shall know neither the day nor the hour when he will return, for it will be as a thief in the night.

We will have no time for preparation. And my question to you this evening is: Will you be ready? When we see one like the Son of Man descending on the clouds of glory, will you be ready to be caught up together with him in the clouds? Do you want to be ready? Then, come! Come, ladies and gentlemen, and kneel here at this altar tonight! Come! Christ is saying to each one of us, *'Behold, I stand at the door and knock; if any man hear my voice and open the door, I will come in to him'* [Rev. 3:20 KJV]. Surely you hear him knocking this evening at the door of your heart; then come! Come! He says, 'Open the door!'"

My heart thumps so loudly in my chest that I glance about nervously, certain others must hear its beating as clearly as I. As weeping men and women file up to kneel, trembling, at the altar, I stare, hypnotized. Deacons make a beeline for the penitents, placing their hands upon their foreheads, praying aloud with them. The murmur of prayers fills the sanctuary. My body develops a clear will of its own, revving up like the engine of a plane preparing for flight or a cat's muscles flexing to pounce upon a canary. My entire body tingles, craving to surrender to the irresistible force, a compulsion that will not be denied. Yet each time I step out for the dramatic stroll to the altar, my mother's controlling hand lays hold of mine. "No," she emphatically states. "You're not old enough yet."

"Please let me go!" I insist. "Jesus is calling to me. Let me go!"

"No, son!" she says in no uncertain terms. "Stay here!" But my body is determined and once again lunges forward. This time, when her rock-firm hand grasps mine, she doesn't release it, and I finally succumb to the greater force, the unyielding grip of my mother, and tremble in my place in the pew.

"You're not old enough," she repeats. "You must wait until you reach the age of accountability." My mother will not relent but continues holding firmly to my arm.

Several years will elapse before I eventually grasp what she means by the enigmatic phrase "age of accountability"—that vague, uncertain time in my adolescence when I (supposedly) would have the mature judgment needed to make a decision of such magnitude.

BIBLE SELECTION

People were bringing little children to Jesus to have him touch them, but the disciples rebuked them. When Jesus saw this, he was indignant. He said to them,

"Let the little children come to me, and do not hinder them, for the kingdom of God belongs to such as these. I tell you the truth, anyone who will not receive the kingdom of God like a little child will never enter it." And he took the children in his arms, put his hands on them and blessed them (Mark 10:13-16 NIV).

REFLECTION

What would have been the outcome, I ask myself today, *if I had been permitted to go up to that altar? If someone had followed and prayed with me on that occasion? Would the Spirit of God have worked a mighty work of commitment in me?* I do not know; I guess I never will.

Over the succeeding years I failed to recognize my increasing self-deception—a truth as obvious as the nose upon my face. That truth was comprised of at least the following components:

1. I was so very blind! There is a God—just look at the trees! Today I see that to believe otherwise is absolutely absurd.
2. The hidden motive for accepting the false premise of atheism was that I might fill that gap with myself. I replaced God as the primary object of my affections. And isn't this a conflict of interest? As the Christian philosopher Dallas Willard observed: "If God is running the universe and has first claim on our lives, guess who isn't running the universe and does not get to have things as they please."[3]
3. I failed to acknowledge in my own heart a link with the divine and eternal—for we know intuitively that we are made for more than this world (Eccl. 3:11). But in order to recognize this we must look beyond our own reflections in the mirror.
4. I failed to accept the validity of other people's lives. Their lives are just as important as mine. My capacity for empathy lay dormant and unused.

In a state of despair brought on by a growing awareness of powerlessness—my inability to fix my increasing problems—finally, in midlife, I reached out to the true God (who most assuredly was *not* me). Continually exasperated at my failure to fix my ballooning problems, in desperation I eventually turned, dear Lord, to you. I finally made it to that altar, completed the journey upon which I had embarked as a child. And I found you there, dear Jesus, waiting patiently. Then you took me up into your arms and granted me a share of your sweet, sweet peace.

Dear God, I cannot thank you enough. And I know that I never shall be able to, for your gift to me is of such enormity that the extent of my appreciation must always remain ineffable; I cannot begin to express it in words.

In the precious name of Jesus Christ my Savior I pray. Amen.

CHAPTER SIX

How I Lost My Best Friend

ONE SUMMER, DADDY HIRED an African-American boy named Billy to work for us, putting him up in a room in our barn. Billy and I were both 11 when he came to stay, and of similar build and temperament—skinny, inquisitive and sensitive. At the time it seemed no color line yet separated us. It was as if the sharp boundaries of what was and wasn't acceptable between the black and white races had not yet fully crystallized within us. We were simply boys tossing the football and recounting personal tales (greatly exaggerated) of unlikely adventure and misadventure. I shared with him my books and watched him pore excitedly over the pages, treating them as if they were rare and beautiful things.

Daddy put us to work hauling hay in from the fields. Billy and I lifted and tossed bales into the back of our pickup truck as my younger brother maneuvered it over the mown grass. A bit of a prankster, one day Billy came upon the carcass of a chicken snake that had been sliced in two by the mowing machine. I was hoisting a bale high above my head, standing with my back to him when, suddenly, he tossed the carcass toward me, screaming, "Snake! Snake!" Not a little startled (a number of local people were killed by snakebite each summer), I immediately dropped the bale and dodged to one side, crying out as the carcass wrapped itself around my bare legs. Then, seeing that it was shredded (and an innocuous chicken snake, at that), I darted an accusing glance at Billy, who had by now broken into a deep belly laugh and was rolling around on the ground. "Ha! Ha! Ha! Gotcha! Gotcha! You old scaredy-cat!" My brother joined in the fun, laughing with him. Not to be outdone, I took the snake's carcass by the tail and tossed it back at Billy. He dodged, then, still laughing, lifted both arms into the air and danced a little jig. "Oh, I'm scared! I'm scared! Look at me, I'm so very scared!"

Then arrived that day in early spring—Billy had been with us about a year by then—when we quarreled so fervently that it left us each with a broken heart. The odd thing is that when I try to recollect the incident today, I vividly remember Billy's reaction to my taunting, especially the deep hurt in his eyes, yet I do not recall the topic of the argument. I know it took place as we were working together beneath the cherry tree in the field beyond the dirt road passing in front of our house. The tree was in full bloom, and the aroma of its blossoms was poignant in the air, a wonder I took for granted at the time. A heated exchange erupted, and the harsh words I used (which can never be taken back) have weighed heavily upon me down through the years.

Now that I think about it, I believe I was resentful of Billy for being far better at something than I (though for the life of me I can't remember what it was). Although I was still a child, envy was already an old nemesis of mine, driving me to sad extremes. I think Billy said something that stuck in my craw, filling me with an anger that was shocking and intense. Impulsively I reached deep within myself, seeking some point of leverage, some instrument to help me prove I was somehow better than him. And the only thing I could come up with, the one thing I could find, was a deeply ingrained notion that I was of a superior race—a beneficiary of a more fortuitous circumstance of birth. And somewhere, somehow, I had learned that one word, one word above all other words, could hurt—yes: the "n" word—and, tragically, this was the weapon I chose to use in retaliation against my friend. "You're a n_____! That's what you are, Billy! You're just a n_____!"

I will never forget what happened next. Billy turned toward me with an expression of such intense and profound hurt that it cut me to the quick. It was a look not unlike that which Caesar must have cast toward Brutus as he mouthed the tragic words, "Et tu, Brute?" It was as if I had done no less than stab my dear friend in the back and he was deeply pained that I would commit such a dastardly deed.

Nevertheless, I would not be deterred from my cruel and spiteful retaliation. I shouted aloud again, "N_____! You're just a n_____!" Billy's whole body recoiled; he dropped his head, turned, and walked slowly away. My heart was grieved when I realized the intensity of the hurt I had wrought upon my friend. But I was on a roll and could not stop myself; a compulsion had taken hold, an obsession that overrode my increasing remorse. "You're just a n_____, Billy! And you will always be!"

From deep within the core of my being a monster arose, a cruel beast that battled against my incipient guilt. I was riding the crest of an overpowering wave of arrogance that lusted for still more and more advantage. That beast raised its grotesque head, roaring in pride at its control, even as my heart melted at the sight of my friend sadly departing. I had crushed him, and I knew it. I had forever lost a friend for whom I cared very deeply. Yet I could not bring myself to utter one single word of apology.

Though Billy remained with us for another month, I never apologized. I kept my distance, and he kept his. Yet the deep hurt I had detected upon his face as I hurled the hateful, vindictive words his way still haunts me to this day. I had done a very cruel thing, yet could not muster the courage to mend my error. Shamefully, the vicious beast I had awakened lived to reign and roar another day.

BIBLE SELECTIONS

The Samaritan woman said to him, "You are a Jew and I am a Samaritan woman. How can you ask me for a drink?" (For Jews do not associate with Samaritans.) Jesus answered her, "If you knew the gift of God and who it is that asks you for a drink, you would have asked him and he would have given you living water."... Just then his disciples returned and were surprised to find him talking with a woman (John 4:9-10, 27 NIV).

In Christ's family there can be no division into Jew and non-Jew, slave and free, male and female. Among us you are all equal. That is, we are all in a common relationship with Jesus Christ (Gal. 3:28 MSG).

REFLECTION

It is the nature of bigotry to erect walls between people. But love cuts a wide swath through prejudice, leaving otherwise insurmountable barriers dismantled in its wake. Today I know that when our Lord suffered, bled and died on Calvary, he did it for every human being on the face of the earth. Just as Christ, sitting by a well in Samaria, engaged in conversation with a Samaritan woman, although *Jews do not associate with Samaritans* (John 4:9), and his disciples on returning *were surprised to find him talking with a woman* (John 4:27), so God's love knows no artificial boundaries between people but cuts decisively through any petty constructs we humans may devise.

Three questions have plagued me throughout my life:

1. Why is it that as a boy I knew the truth—that the local customs that implied that black people were not as good

as white people were based on a lie—yet I followed along without question? I recall toilets marked "For Coloreds Only"; African-Americans were forbidden, as well, from attending the same public schools as whites. It was likewise with the churches (sadly, in many instances it remains so today). Yet, amazingly, I consented without open protest to these customs!

2. And why is it that, although I knew the truth, I intentionally used that lie to hurt another human being—when I broke Billy's heart?

3. And why is it that it took me several decades to allow the truth to seep into the depths of my being, to redefine my personality so that I could honestly say that I love all people equally, regardless of race, gender, nationality or any other artificial boundary?

The answer to those questions, I realize today, is that I did not yet know the transformational power of Jesus Christ—it took his power to drain me of the last vestiges of hypocrisy and bigotry. Until I knew the Lord, I was unable to allow that truth to permeate my inner being and transform me; I was unable to truly feel and demonstrate sincere love for another human being (or even for myself, for that matter). Until I would accept Christ's love and love him in return, and in loving him, love all people everywhere, I remained enchained by the prejudices I had unwittingly acquired as a youth. I learned how to love by accepting the Lord's love for myself, and I learned how to forgive by accepting his forgiveness.

Lord, how could you ever forgive the things I did, the hurt I brought upon you by the cruel way I treated others? My misery brought harm to many as I projected my inner fears and self-hatred onto those around me, many of whom cared for me.

"Dear Lord," I asked when I was first saved, "can you really forgive me for those ugly deeds of my past?" Your reply was to look on me with a wondrous, all-embracing love. Then I remembered that you are my God, not just another person; you are the Lord; you are my Creator; and you love me with a deep and everlasting love, the depths of which I cannot plumb (Eph. 3:19). And I am overcome with thanksgiving.

In the precious name of Jesus Christ my Savior I pray. Amen.

CHAPTER SEVEN

The Genesis of Atheism

AT AGE 12 I HIT UPON a discovery that enchanted me, eventually leading me away from my early homage to God. It was an idea—quite an old one, really, though one very new to me—which I gleaned from the pages of two books, county library copies of Charles Darwin's *On the Origin of Species* and *The Descent of Man*. I secreted these books away to my hideout in the woods where, sprawled face down for hours upon the autumn leaves, I traced Darwin's etchings with my fingers, marveling at the range of species he discovered upon the Galapagos Islands. Then one day, mysteriously, a light clicked on in my mind as I suddenly grasped his point and a whole new world opened up before me. It all seemed so very obvious at the time!

While Darwin made it clear in his writings that he wasn't an atheist, in the course of my varied searching I encountered the terms "evolution," "Darwinism" and "atheism" in association again and again, as if the understanding of one concept opened the door to another. I had never met an evolutionist. Due to my very limited life experience, I found it difficult to believe such people existed at all beyond the pages of my books! And, though I surely knew the notion was absurd, it seemed that the authors were not composed of flesh and blood at all, but rather of some higher, ethereal substance.

As I gazed about my father's 200-acre farm, Darwin's theory of the natural selection of the species began to make sense to me. Living close to nature, I was awestruck daily, witnessing miracles such as cattle giving birth. I was integrally involved, helping more than once to turn a calf around within its mother's womb to ensure it would emerge safely. I watched intrigued as we corralled our prize Angus bull, pairing him one at a time with selected cows so their calves would be of preferred stock. In time I concluded that the similarities between people and the various animal species could not be denied and must mean that all species, over eons, evolved from a common ancestor. As the pieces of the puzzle seemed to come together, I was excited. It was a very heady experience, indeed!

My belief in God, however, was not immediately threatened; if anything, it was strengthened! For I concluded that such an intriguing plan could only have come about through the action of an omnipotent, omniscient Intelligence. There in my early adolescence, I hit upon the rationale of Methodist theologian E. Stanley Jones:

> About evolution. When you say that "resident forces" are capable of producing the universe, we ask: How could resident forces move toward intelligent ends without being intelligent?... You smuggle God into the process and then say He is not necessary! But God would be as necessary for evolution as for a once-for-all creation. Which takes the more intelligence—to strike a billiard ball straight into the pocket at one stroke, or to strike a ball, which in turn strikes another, and that another, and that another, until the last one goes into the pocket? Obviously, the latter stroke.[4]

Jones' reasoning made perfect sense to me, but then I encountered British philosopher Bertrand Russell's essay, "Why I am Not a Christian." And it was this intriguing paper that planted within me the seeds of atheism.

> It is maintained that everything we see in this world has a cause, and as you go back in the chain of causes further and further you must come to a First Cause, and to that First Cause you give the name of God.... You can see that the argument that there must be a First Cause is one that cannot have any validity. I may say that when I was a young man, and was debating these questions very seriously in my mind, I for a long time accepted the argument of the First Cause, until one day, at the age of 18, I read John Stuart Mill's *Autobiography*, and I there found this sentence: "My father taught me that the question, 'Who made me?' cannot be answered, since it immediately suggests the further question, 'Who made God?'" That very simple sentence showed me, as I still think, the fallacy in the argument of the First Cause. If everything must have a cause, then God must have a cause. If there can be anything without a cause, it may

just as well be the world as God, so that there cannot be any
validity in that argument.[5]

Reading this passage, a surge of adrenaline shot through me, a
magnificently thrilling sensation—along with a great dose of daredevil-like
haughtiness. *Do I dare?* I asked myself. *Do I dare permit my mind to tread
through such treacherous terrain, for such conjecture is condemned by everyone I
know?* From a religious perspective, I lived in a very homogenous community.
Not only were all the people I knew professing Christians, but they were all
Protestant—in fact, they were primarily either Baptist or Methodist.

Then, when at 13 I read for the first time Karl Marx's comments debasing
religion as "the opiate of the masses," my mind flew to such heights of
arrogance I could feel my lower lip curling up into a sneer. The contempt I
felt for those around me may not have been evident to them, but I recall
with exceeding clarity the scorn that I felt. I looked down upon my parents
with increasing disdain. I feel almost nauseous as I reflect on this today, but
I am determined to write the truth about my past, and this is it. Seeing my
parents pore studiously over the Sunday school lesson before church and
then observing them sitting in the pews, listening attentively to the minister,
my attitude grew more and more patronizing!

Few things are as intoxicating as a teenager's first taste of arrogance,
and few things become addictive as quickly. Recovering cocaine and heroin
addicts have told me that the substance abuser's first chemical high carries
such a kick that one often becomes addicted after the very first use—and
that every use of the drug thereafter is an effort to recapture the pleasure of
that first high. The addict never succeeds in doing so, yet never ceases trying.
So it was that I relished the sheer pleasure of my condescension toward those
about me.

As I began to reframe my worldview according to this newly acquired
perspective, I set out to describe a world in which there is no God. *If we
humans have not yet unraveled the mystery of precisely how our world came into
being without a creator, we will—just give us time,* I reasoned. *For as surely as
we found a vaccine for polio and invented a machine in which to fly, so we will
solve this puzzle, also.* My chest swelled with pride at the revelation of my
newfound god, humankind, for my new object of worship was none other
than that sample of humanity to whom I was closest; my new god, you see,
was none other than—myself!

This is a predictable outcome. As E. Stanley Jones observed:

> When God is no longer the center, then we become the center—we become [our god].... Aldous Huxley says, "One strange result of scientific progress has been the reversion of monotheism to local idolatries." And when those "local idolatries" are not state and race and class—which are the self writ large—then they are just the personal self. When we lose God, then we become [our god].[6]

It is an extremely exhilarating experience to make the leap from acceptance of the true God to playing the role in one's own life. Gloating all the way, I took the reins of my life into my own hands and placed myself upon an exceedingly high pedestal.

Dallas Willard informs us:

> Human beings have always known there is a God and have some degree of understanding of who he is and what he is like (Rom. 1:19-20). Actually, they still do. But they were not pleased that he should have the place in the universe that he does have merely because he is who he is.... As Augustine saw clearly, God being God offends human pride. *If God is running the universe and has first claim on our lives, guess who isn't running the universe and does not get to have things as they please.*[7] (emphasis mine)

I made the leap to atheism, I believe, partly because Satan tempted me by persuading me that the relationship I had with God as a child was only a delusion—that God had never really been with me, after all. Today I recognize that a supernatural agent must have been at work, for my conscious recollection of the role God played in my early life is very vivid. In the face of this incontrovertible fact—my early intimacy with God—I know that the denial of it only a few years later is not something I could have done if Satan had not deceived me.

However, my own egotism also most assuredly played a major role: *[E]ach one is tempted when, by his own evil desire, he is dragged away and enticed. Then, after desire has conceived, it gives birth to sin; and sin, when it is full-grown, gives birth to death* (James 1:14-15 NIV).

My new self-centered outlook quickly began to impact my relationships with the people who loved me. As my dad sought increasingly to mold me into his vision of what a young man should be, I rebelled more and more. *If it doesn't suit me, I won't have it!* I decided, and I refused to comply with my father's wishes. This behavior by itself was not unique—I had been there many times—but there was this difference: this time I *openly* defied him, that is I overtly, stubbornly refused to give in. The other difference lay in what happened afterwards.

Shortly after I turned 14, I came in from the fields at 2 p.m. one day without permission. Sprawling across my bed, I plunged back into a book I had been reading, which had been holding me spellbound. My mother suddenly appeared in the doorway, staring in at me as if incredulous of my behavior, while my head remained buried in the book. *Oh, no,* I thought. *I've been found out.* I had never done such a brazen thing before. I glanced up at her questioningly, wondering what she would do.

But my mother, who shared my love for books, smiled as if we had a mutual secret and said, "It's alright. Go ahead and finish your book." Breathing a huge sigh of relief, I returned to my reading as she closed the door.

Yet an hour later, the door swung wide and there stood Daddy in his work overalls, fierce anger blazing from his eyes. "You lazy.... Come on out here in the yard. Go get a switch and bring it to me right now!"

Scowling to myself, I lay the book aside and dragged myself reluctantly out into the backyard where Daddy stood watching me, glaring. Mama was by his side, gazing helplessly down at the ground.

"Where's that switch I told you to get?" Daddy snapped.

Abruptly, as if it had a life of its own, defiance rose in me in a way I had never felt before. I became resolute. *I've had enough of this!* I said to myself. *I'm 14 now. I don't have to take this anymore!* I remained silent.

"Why did you leave your work and come back to the house?" Daddy demanded.

"Mama said it was okay," I replied.

Daddy glanced at Mama, and Mama shot me back an expression that jarred me. I had certainly not expected her reaction; her glance revealed disappointment and accused me of betrayal. I knew I was in deep trouble. But it had never occurred to me that I should not tell Daddy. I didn't realize they had secrets. Her look of resentment pained me greatly.

Cussing, Daddy angrily snatched off a switch from the bush in our backyard and began lashing out at my back, arms, and legs. But I was a strapping boy by now, over six feet tall, and the licks seemed to bounce off me—they stung little. I stood unmoving, unresisting, and took my licking silently. Finally, tired of swinging at me, frustrated at my unrepentant behavior, Daddy stomped off. "Now go back and finish your work," he growled as he headed back to the fields.

Moments later, while I was bent over the bathroom sink, washing my face, I looked up to see Mama standing in the doorway, that same confusing look on her face—but this time, mixed with the disappointment I also sensed fear. It was clear I had disappointed her—I did so unknowingly, but this seemed to make no difference. I didn't know what to do.

"Don't you ever, ever come between me and your daddy again!" she said in a steady, low voice. "Never again!" With a grunt, she turned her back and left, giving me no chance to explain. Her manner was barren of love. It was as if she had chosen between Daddy and me, and Daddy had won. My heart sank. The message came through loud and clear: My mother—whom I had always seen as my consolation partner, the one who had always stood by me in my frequent confrontations with my father—had abandoned me.

I was stunned! It was as if someone had thrown scalding water in my face! My mind reeled. What I remember most is the sense of absolute abandonment I felt. I had already given up God; to me, he no longer existed. And now I felt I had lost both my father and my mother as well! (That is how I irrationally viewed it at the time.) I felt completely alone in the world.

Over the next few days I refused to talk to my dad, though he, my three younger brothers and I were often together at meals or working side by side in the fields. It was evident he was very annoyed; yet he never specifically addressed the situation. I was growing more and more aware that I would have to live my life by myself and for myself, to find the answers to all of life's questions on my own. It would be a difficult struggle—just me against the world. But I knew beyond a shadow of a doubt that I would ultimately succeed!

I never told a soul about my newfound atheism. I hid my secret pretty well. Today people tell me they saw me at the time as shy and withdrawn, a quiet lad. Yet I know that I was bathing in self-adulation! I was all alone with my secret that I had taken the time to look into the matter and found that there is no God. However, I found it a very lonely experience. For up until now, I had often spoken with God; he had been my best friend. I didn't realize he was still around, patiently waiting for me to renew the relationship, that I intentionally had chosen to break the association, and that it was an entirely unilateral act. I had no hint as yet of the despair that awaited me as a result of my conscious decision to discard my faith—what Kierkegaard called "sin against the Holy Spirit":

> The sin of abandoning Christianity *modo ponendo* [positively], of declaring it to be untruth—this is sin against the Holy Spirit. Here the self is at the height of despair: it not only throws all of Christianity aside, but makes it out to be lies and falsehood—what a stupendously despairing conception such a self must have of itself![8]

BIBLE SELECTION

The poor, deluded fool feeds on ashes.
He is trusting something that can give him
no hope at all. Yet he cannot bring himself to ask,
"Is this thing, this idol that I'm holding in my hand, a lie?" (Isa. 44:20 NLT).

REFLECTION

Most of us have some unpleasant memory upon which we prefer not to dwell. For we have learned through experience that if we do so, the memory will take on a life of its own, eating at us, causing us great pain. Sometimes it is regret over a deed done or left undone which has marred us permanently, though we realize that there is no way to reverse the harm that has been done; we cannot undo the past.

Left unexamined and unacknowledged, however, such a memory will eat a hole in our gut, hurting us even more—emotionally, spiritually and even physically. David was well aware of this. He writes: *When I refused to confess my sin I was weak and miserable, and I groaned all day long. Day and night, [God,] your hand of discipline was heavy on me. My strength evaporated like water in the summer heat* (Ps. 32:3-4 NLT).

Such incidents in our past—be they little or large in the final scale of things—cast a shadow upon all that follows after and can affect other people, many of them very close and dear to us. The repercussions, in turn, hurt us further, to the extent that we blame ourselves and our own faulty choices for the hurtful consequences—the toll taken upon our loved ones. I don't know what your traumatic memory may be, but I know very well my own—David wrote of it: *The fool says in his heart, "There is no God"* (Ps. 14:1 NIV); it is the conscious choice I made in my teens to become an atheist. The consequences of that choice followed me down through the years, leaving a lasting, harmful imprint upon all who depended on me. Hurtful damage was done that I can never undo.

The toll upon my ex-wife and children has been horrendous. It would be a long time before I would experience the deliverance David writes about: *Finally I confessed all my sins to you and stopped trying to hide them. I said to myself, "I will confess my rebellion to the Lord." And you forgave me! All my guilt is gone* (Ps. 32:5 NLT).

Lord, I have laid my burden at your feet, admitted my gross mistakes, the faulty conclusions at which I arrived, especially the grievous error that you do not exist. The realization that you do exist—that I had been wrong all along—has shaken me to the very core of my being. Leaving you out of the equation for so many years, it is no wonder that things turned out so badly. I floundered like a fish out of water, for I was created to serve you, Lord, yet I was attempting to live my life without taking you into account. Thank you for a second chance, for your full forgiveness and continuing love.

In the precious name of Jesus Christ my Savior I pray. Amen.

CHAPTER EIGHT

The Baptismal Lie

BY THE TIME I TURNED 16, my early childhood obsession to kneel at the altar had become a distant memory. Though I continued to attend church services with my family, I did so only to appease my parents. While I had openly defied them in proportionally smaller things, to defy them in this, I felt, would be too much; I knew it would hurt them immensely. Despite our differences, I loved them dearly and did not want to cause them this kind of pain.

But there came a day when accompanying my parents to church was no longer enough; they longed for my spiritual salvation. In their view I had now passed that elusive "age of accountability" when a child is presumed to be mature enough to make an informed decision for Christ. They wanted me to do what I had longed to do as a small child: go forward to the altar, kneel, permit the preacher to pray with me, then be baptized in the old-fashioned way. They let me know this through several far-from-subtle hints. When these failed, they confronted me openly, and I was running out of excuses.

But what they did not know—because I had not gotten up the courage or wherewithal to tell them (or anyone else for that matter)—was that I had meanwhile become a full-blown, self-described atheist.

In retrospect I can see three primary reasons why I kept my new-found atheism a secret:

1. I did not want to hurt my parents' feelings. Despite my arrogant conclusion that I was of far superior intelligence to them (as well as to everyone else in our rural community)—that I and I alone was in possession of "the truth," while their beliefs were mere fantasy—I loved my parents very much and didn't wish to hurt them. I really believed that if they knew my true feelings, it would crush them.
2. I could not envision a scenario in which I could confront them with my point of view.

3. At bottom, I was afraid. The prospect of the storm in my family that I was convinced would follow such a revelation was too much for me to handle. Avoidance, therefore, seemed the best course of action, and this is the alternative I chose.

But an immediate challenge loomed: how was I ever going to get past the present hurdle—my parents' obsession with me being saved? The whole issue was about to come to a head. The summer after I turned 16, a series of revival meetings were held at our country church, and it soon became evident that my parents had taken matters into their own hands.

On the first night, as the altar call was sounded and those feeling "the call of the Holy Ghost" went forward to kneel, I suddenly became aware that the preacher was looking directly at me. I stared down at my feet. I hadn't believed a word of what he had said and was determined not to be moved. As people continued to file up to the altar, the preacher made a beeline for me where I was standing beside my parents at a center pew. Taking my arm, the large, ruddy-faced man asked in a hushed voice, "Son, are you ready tonight to give your heart to the Lord?"

"No, sir," I replied nervously.

Undeterred, he smiled patiently at me. I glanced at my parents, whose expectancy was quite obvious, and everything quickly became crystal clear: they had conspired with the minister! I was very annoyed.

"Why not tonight?" asked the minister.

"I'm just not ready, sir," I responded. He moved on.

What in the world am I going to do? I wondered. *I can't tell my parents the truth. They would never understand! Yet I won't pray to a God whom I know doesn't exist. What in the world am I going to do?*

The next day seemed full of tension so thick you could cut it with a knife. All day I dreaded the evening, knowing the events of the night before were certain to be repeated. All alone, I carried a crushing weight. Though I longed to share the burden, I could think of no one in whom I could confide. I tried to beg out of the evening service, but my parents wouldn't permit it. *I can't go on like this,* I worried. *I don't know what to do.*

That night the preacher spoke on the Apocalypse, and the account struck me as absurd. *Why can't they see how ridiculous it all is?* I asked myself. *A battle between good and evil—one side first getting the upper hand, then the other—*

with the human soul as the bizarre battleground! Or it's like a huge chess game—the good competing with the bad. We humans are the chess pieces moved about on a cosmic game board, yet the omnipotent forces, rather than manipulating the pieces as in a proper game, merely stand by watching, waiting to see what choices we people will make. The devil whispers slyly, "Come on over here. I will give you such pleasure."

"How very ridiculous!" I muttered beneath my breath.

As he did the night before, when the altar call sounded and the congregation reverently stood, the preacher took his calculated walk down the aisle. *Like a ferocious beast stalking his prey,* I thought. I stared down at the floor. *Oh, please! No! I don't want to go through this again!* But there he was standing next to me. I glanced at my parents and saw anticipation writ large upon their faces. Then for the first time I noticed others in the congregation stealing glances in our direction. I frowned. *How big a conspiracy is this?*

The minister gripped my arm firmly. "Son, tonight are you ready to give your heart to Jesus?"

"No, sir. I'm not."

"What are you waiting on, son? The Lord is longing for you." He nodded at my parents. I grimaced; I was so annoyed!

The following day was torturous. *I have to live in this house, in this community. What in the world am I going to do?* Then I hit upon an idea: *I know! I know! I'll just go through the motions, and no one will ever know the difference! That will get both the preacher and my parents off my back once and for all.* I grinned mischievously. *I am so clever,* I decided, *so very clever. If I can just pull this off!*

So that night as the preacher took my arm and asked me once again, "Are you ready to give your heart to the Lord?" I instantly replied, "Yes, sir. I will accept it." He smiled, clearly greatly relieved. *(I'll just say, "I accept it,"* I thought to myself, *not that I believe it—because I don't. Then it won't be a complete lie.)* As the preacher led me by the arm to the altar, it seemed the eyes of everyone in the congregation were fixed upon me. It was as if the next act in a continuing drama was now unfolding.

As the large man knelt and sincerely prayed for my soul, I thought, *I am so shrewd, so very calculating. I have them eating out of the palm of my hands. They think I'm being saved, but it's just a charade to get them off my back. They will never know the difference, these simpletons. These idiots! They are seeing only what they want to see. It will never occur to them that I'm only pretending, for they could never imagine such a thing.*

The water baptism was set to take place the following Sunday afternoon at an abandoned gravel pit, which, after the spring rains, had enlarged into a pond. As the day drew nearer, I dreaded the event, knowing what a masquerade it was going to be; then, oddly, I began to gloat, for I found I had become something of a star. It was my big day! "Congratulations, son! You're making a big decision. You're taking a significant step," said my uncles and aunts and neighbors.

I took full advantage of the circumstances to exult. In my sick arrogance, I looked at myself as a god whose subjects were doing his bidding, carrying out their individual roles. *They're so predictable, these simple people whose religion is but a sedative to get them through their days. Why don't they open up their eyes and take a look around themselves? They will see there is no God. They conclude he is invisible so they can buy into their own absurd delusions. It never occurs to them that they describe him as invisible so they can hide the truth that he doesn't even exist. No, that would be too obvious!* How I looked down on them. I had no idea I had set myself up as my own god—that it was I myself I worshiped, I myself I served. I perceived myself as beyond time and place, like a deity, for I felt there was no other who was as wise as I. That Sunday morning, however, there was one who appeared to be getting suspicious.

As he finished the sermon, the preacher plucked his latest trophies one by one from the pews—the 14 people to be baptized later in the day. All were teenagers except two, a backslidden, middle-aged alcoholic and a recalcitrant great-grandfather facing imminent death from cancer.

Finally leading me to the altar, he asked, "Son, do you believe Jesus Christ died for your sins and today is interceding with the Father on your behalf?"

Like clockwork I responded glibly, "I accept it."

This time, however, the preacher was not to be so easily fooled. "But do you believe it?" he countered.

Not to be deterred, I responded: "I said, 'I accept it.'"

His eyes flashed, and a look of obvious annoyance showed on his face. "You *accept* it?" he repeated. "But I'm asking you, boy, do you *believe* it?" This time I was silent. The minister shook his head in exasperation and finally moved on. I stared down at my hands, frozen, wondering if I had been found out.

That afternoon, amidst a cappella hymns of jubilation, the preacher led us one by one by the hand into the chilly, clear pond water. As I waded out, a warm breeze blew up and I felt as if I were in a kind of fantasyland in which everyone was playing an assumed role. *I'm caught in limbo,* I said to myself, *in some kind of no-man's-land between reality and a contrived past—a perspective we've all invented to assuage our consciences because we feel so guilty over past or imagined sins. We play these parts, these silly roles we've prescribed for ourselves, to appease deep-seated feelings of remorse. Today I'm going through an ancient ritual so I will not be punished for failing to fulfill a role I have been assigned—a part which I do not seek or desire. What other purpose can this farcical playacting possibly serve?*

Standing beside me in the waist-deep water, the minister pleaded, "Son, do you now believe Jesus Christ died for your sins so you may live again? Do you confess with your mouth that Jesus Christ is Lord, and believe in your heart that God raised him from the dead?"

I frowned and replied as I had done all along, "I accept it," then added beneath my breath, "so that you will finally leave me alone!"

He grimaced. "But do you *believe*?" he repeated.

Determined to play the role out to its bitter end, I said again "I accept it."

Still clearly irritated, but perhaps just wanting to get the deed behind him once and for all, the preacher dunked me backwards into the cool water. "I baptize you in the name of the Father and of the Son and of the Holy Ghost," he hastily recited, then quickly brought me up out of the water. It was as if a breeze blew down from off an icy peak, such a chill shot through me.

What was it that so caught me up at that moment that I felt cleaner than I had ever felt before? Was it simply the rush of cool pond water across my face, or was God the Holy Spirit somehow involved? After sincerely surrendering to Christ 23 years later, I often wondered what the Lord thought of me at that instant as I went through the motions of accepting him as my God and Savior just to get those people off my back!

BIBLE SELECTION

Do not deceive yourselves. If any one of you thinks he is wise by the standards of this age, he should become a "fool" so that he may become wise. For the wisdom of this world is foolishness in God's sight. As it is written: "He catches the wise in their craftiness"; and again, "The Lord knows that the thoughts of the wise are futile" (1 Cor. 3:18-20 NIV).

REFLECTION_____

Reflecting back across 43 years to the event of my feigned conversion at age 16, I marvel at how precariously my soul hung in the balance—the inevitable consequence of succumbing to the temptation of self-pride. From that moment on, I stood alone against all the evil and sorrow I was to encounter in the world. (At the time I had no idea of the depth of degradation that would hold me hostage—a direct result of the natural human tendency to operate on self-will.)

While counseling men and women in my Salvation Army ministry, I see the same course of action repeated again and again—people making the same mistake I did, choosing self-adoration over love of the Lord out of doubt that there is a true God. As the Big Book of Alcoholics Anonymous puts it:

> We were bothered with the thought that faith and dependence upon a Power beyond ourselves was somewhat weak, even cowardly. We looked upon this world of warring individuals, warring theological systems, and inexplicable calamity, with deep skepticism. We looked askance at many individuals who claimed to be godly. How could a Supreme Being have anything to do with it all? And who could comprehend a Supreme Being anyhow?[9]

I have come to see that millions of people step off into the slippery terrain of prideful early adulthood following this same mistaken way of thinking, oblivious that it is the temptation to glorify themselves that is really behind it all. Because self-adulation is so very seductive—as well as addictive— tragically, many die before they learn to think correctly. Having chosen to deny that there is a true God, they conclude it is themselves they must please, themselves upon whom they must depend, themselves whom they must ply with gifts of all kinds. And the more they do so, the more they believe it to be true, for it is a self-perpetuating spiral upon which they have embarked, one that develops a momentum of its own. They stubbornly persist in this manner until they run into deep trouble, then find they have insufficient resources within themselves to deal with the problems incurred in daily living. Turning now to other recourses and finding them also insufficient, the only real choice that remains before them is whether to finally turn to God or slip off into insanity—with perhaps hell itself awaiting on the other side of the huge divide!

Dear God, I pray for all the youth of the world. As they move into adulthood with its numerous challenges, I pray that they turn to you for guidance in making the difficult choices of life. You love them so dearly and lovingly seek their companionship. When I was in their shoes, I turned down your offer of divine counsel and set out on my life journey with only my fragile, limited mind as a resource—and consequently I took the wrong steps again and again. Fortunately, dear God, I did not die in my sins—though I came perilously close! It was as if your angel was looking after me; you cared for me, and if I had died in that state I would never have had the opportunity to reciprocate your abundant love. I thank you, dear Lord, for your infinite patience with me.

In the precious name of Jesus Christ my Savior I pray. Amen.

PART II
THE MILITARY

CHAPTER NINE

Death's New Face

THE WAIL OF THE SIREN CUTS through our consciousness like a razor-sharp, twisting knife, rapidly followed by bare feet slapping the floor as the first of the mortar rounds strike: "Ka-whump! Ka-whump!" It is October 1967, and at the Bien Hoa Air Base, the Republic of Vietnam, the whole hooch trembles as the rolling thunder follows us down the hall.

Clad only in briefs and boxers, we hurl headlong into the night, frantically leaping for the cave of sandbags half-buried beyond our hooch. There, crouching together in the darkness, our arms clasped tightly about our legs, we shudder from our fear. We are brothers bound closely together by this common experience, a bond solid and unique. The shells whistle through the sky, exploding as they strike, roaring ever louder and louder, finally sounding just yards away. They slice the air, pounding the earth like gigantic serpents lunging at their prey or runaway trains ramming a mountainside. "God, help us!" screams the man next to me, his knees slapping mine spasmodically.

But I grimace, for I see myself as far superior to him. *Only the weak of will and mind need cling to that old myth,* I think to myself, for years have passed since I believed in God. Cries of terrified men mingle with the blare of sirens. I shudder. Then—abruptly—dead silence! The only sound is our rapid breathing amidst the sporadic screams.

Moments later, shirt unbuttoned, shoes unlaced, I cling to the side of an ambulance tearing through the streets of the compound, searching out the source of all the screaming and crying. The radio crackles with static as we listen carefully for our instructions. Panicky men suddenly materialize from the darkness, waving their arms wildly in the glare of our headlights. "Over here! Over here!" they shout. Then, from another direction, "There're several down beyond this hooch." Soaring into the darkness we spot them: a dozen young men in their underclothes, bodies soaked with blood, twisted in an unnatural fashion. Some are motionless, eyes frozen in great stares of disbelief, faces twisted as if in excruciating pain. Yet some are moving, groaning, shivering, tugging on the blankets that we fling across them.

More ambulances pull in behind us as we work methodically under the guidance of the physicians: "Take this one directly to the operating room. Here, put this on him. Bandage that arm! Go gently. Go gently, now."

Like automatons, unmoved and unthinking, we are very competent, not allowing our emotions to interfere with the performance of our duties—for these are desperate, life-saving moments. Squinting, making the most of the artificial light, we suddenly note that our fingers are functioning independently of our minds—or seem to be—rapidly wrapping, tying, hoisting, carrying. We are surprised at how efficient we are.

Next, huddled down low in the back of the ambulance cutting through the moonlight toward the dispensary, I wipe the forehead of the young man I am holding. "If I die," he tells me, "please tell my sister Kathy how brave I was, how unafraid, and that I'm sorry we argued when I was home in November." He begins to blubber, tears gushing, and I know he feels ashamed at losing his composure. "And tell my mama how much I love her."

As he sobs, blood soaks the bandage about his chest; I adjust it as best I can, wondering what I should say. "Matt, don't worry. You're not going to die—I'm sure of it. You'll be telling them yourself soon. I know you will!" I quake from my own fear as well as exasperation over my helplessness in the face of the situation.

As his sobs continue, I suddenly feel ashamed and look away. I am a product of my culture; a seed was planted in me when I was a child, a notion that a boy who cries is a baby, not a man. *Matt's a sissy, a girl— he should be ashamed!* Now, surrounded by so much death and fear and horror, I determine that crying (which for me is the equivalent of losing control) is the last thing I will do. Matt's sobbing persists involuntarily and I recoil in disgust. I open my mouth to instruct him: *Matt, be a man! Stop blubbering like a baby!* The words well up from deep inside me like water spouting forth from a geyser. Yet, at the last moment I halt them, barring the words from escaping my lips.

The siren blares again, the rounds slashing the air like a cold and hungry sword, unyielding and uncaring. Then comes a slapping, deafening roar— "Ka-whump! Ka-whump!"—as shells maul the earth like a tiger tearing at its prey, slicing, gouging, cutting, ripping. They hit once, twice, three times around us, the sound interspersed amidst the chaotic screams and the roaring of the vehicles. Shrapnel soars overhead as the ambulance plows through the compound, bearing the groaning and sobbing wounded.

The ambulance stops abruptly before the dispensary and we leap to the ground. Grabbing one end of a stretcher, then another, we gently lower our comrades to the earth. A remarkable scene meets my eyes. Working by artificial light, the doctors separate the dead and dying from those not yet mortally wounded. A dozen or so motionless bodies, some of them still breathing, lie to one side, blatantly ignored. "Move the corpses over there. Make room for these new wounded," a sergeant commands. And so we do.

My gaze settles upon the eyes of the young, dead man whose arms I grasp as I swing him off to one side. His eyes are open and as blue as the sky on a clear Southern day. He's my age, just 21. *Does he leave caring parents, brothers, sisters, or perhaps a girlfriend behind? What did he think when he signed up? Did he expect to die?* The thoughts flash through my mind.

I see myself suddenly lying next to him; I imagine what it must be like passing from life into death. *Is it much like falling asleep, just slipping off into unconsciousness, to never wake again? Is it as wordless and passive as all that? Is it a welcome repose, like a deep, sound sleep on a cold, rainy morning, from which you dread being awakened?* Because I do not believe in God, for me there exists no answer for death—rather death simply marks the cessation of living. It follows that dying is much like falling into a comfortable, deep sleep from which one is never aroused.

Mulling over this thought, I shudder. *I mustn't allow myself to go there! I can't go there! I can't!* At some level I realize that if there is no meaning to death, then it logically follows that there is no meaning to life, no purpose at all for my existence; I am but a biological accident and no more. Abruptly, a defense mechanism kicks in. I close the thought. I go numb.

As we move one body, then another, off to the side, an awareness of the absurdity, the grotesqueness of it all, falls over me, and I am stunned. Just an hour ago these were living, laughing, vibrant young men; but now they are no more than sticks of wood, planks of lumber, and practically demands that they be tossed aside to make room for the breathing.

Minutes later, as we barrel again down the streets of the compound, another volley cracks the blackness. Then quite suddenly I am aware that I am numb, that I have become as unfeeling as the dead men I hold. I am no longer afraid, nor can I be. To my surprise, this realization as well does not disturb me. It is okay that I cannot feel, that I am emotionless, not giving in to terror or to shame. I believe this is the way a man must be—it is as natural as eating or drinking. The radio crackles again; the words catch my attention. The scene of the latest carnage is my hooch!

As the ambulance screeches to a halt, I am astounded at what I see: the bunker where I had hunkered for protection against the initial onslaught of the night has been blown to smithereens! The broken, riven bodies we see in the glow of the headlights are those of my hooch mates, my friends with whom I only yesterday played cards, traded jokes, shared a beer!

Taking in the scene, I freeze. I feel I am about to lose my composure—to scream and cry out at the top of my lungs in protest, to sob like a baby—when my new friend, stoicism, in what I understand as a most gracious act of charity, steps into my mind, shuts the door upon my emotions and securely locks it.

Now I am able to move among my dear friends smoothly, unemotionally, as if in a dream, securing their spilling entrails, halting the gushing blood, efficiently hoisting them onto the stretchers. Lifting and moving and bandaging them, I recognize Bill and Steve and Jim and Mark. As we carry them, I address them by their names. Some answer, yet some do not, and cannot for all time. Moments later, speeding back through the darkness, several of the men are sobbing, and not just the wounded, yet I am not one of them. I am cold, completely numb, protected from the fear, sheltered from the grief. *I will never give in to it,* I tell myself. *Never! For I am too big of a man!*

BIBLE SELECTION _____

Listen! The Lord's arm is not too weak to save you, nor his ear too deaf to hear you call. It's your sins that have cut you off from God. Because of your sins, he has turned away and will not listen anymore.

So there is no justice among us, and we know nothing about right living. We look for light but find only darkness. We look for bright skies but walk in gloom. We grope like the blind along a wall, feeling our way like people without eyes. Even at brightest noontime, we stumble as though it were dark. Among the living, we are like the dead. We growl like hungry bears; we moan like mournful doves. We look for justice, but it never comes. We look for rescue, but it is far away from us. For our sins are piled up before God and testify against us (Isa. 59:1-2, 9-12 NLT).

REFLECTION_____

Looking back across the years on my experience during the war, I recognize that my trepidation as I watched others dying about me arose from my faulty conception of death. To me at the time, death was no more than a departure from this temporal existence, a disappearance of life, a vanishing into nonexistence.

One of my most horrifying nightmares during my years as an atheist was a continual replay of a scene I viewed in a movie somewhere: a group of people are making their way up a steep mountain trail when one slips suddenly on a loose pebble and tumbles, screaming, over the cliff edge to his death. The others peer nervously over the side and grimace, each grateful that he is not the one who has fallen, then resignedly resume their trek up the mountainside.

What troubled me was the seemingly senseless and random nature of the incident. What caused one climber to fall to his death and not another? At the time, I put such a thing down to pure chance, concluding there was no meaning to this man's life—or his death—and that all of life consequentially is just as meaningless. It was my terror at the thought that both life and death are senseless that was the real reason for my despair.

I loved life and had no desire to give it up. But it's a cold, cold world when it is perceived only by the five senses. I have since learned there is another sense we all possess which is far superior to the other five. It lies within the spiritual plane and springs from the heart: *For who knows a person's thoughts except that person's own spirit within? In the same way no one knows the thoughts of God except the Spirit of God. We have not received the spirit of the world but the Spirit who is from God, that we may understand what God has freely given us* (1 Cor. 2:11-12 TNIV).

The terror I felt during the war, which was played out in my recurring fears over the decades, sprang from a conflict at the very core of my being—a battle between that which I sensed intuitively in the spiritual plane and that which I grasped consciously via the five senses (which I long believed were the only reliable gauge). No words ever uttered are truer than these: *I have seen the burden God has laid on men. He has made everything beautiful in its time. He has also set eternity in the hearts of men; yet they cannot fathom what God has done from beginning to end* (Eccl. 3:10-11 NIV).

In denying this hint of eternity that God implanted in my heart (as he has in the hearts of people everywhere), I put myself at odds with a dear and distinct truth: there is more to life than what this world has to offer.

Dear Lord, since I gave you my heart, you have shown me through experience, as well as through your Word, that you are with your children in times of distress. I have learned to lean on you in the best of times as well as the worst of times. Your rock-solid presence guiding me, strengthening me, and loving me is a gift for which I can never thank you enough.

In the precious name of Jesus Christ my Savior I pray. Amen.

CHAPTER TEN

Intimations of Despair

ONE MOMENT IS STUCK IN my mind for all time, an image etched for all eternity. It's the image of one of my cohorts, one who lived in the same hooch as me, a red-haired young man whose name I do not remember. In my memory he is 30. I came upon him in the dispensary lobby late on one of those nights that never seemed to end, when the mortar rounds were sounding ceaselessly, leaving bloody bodies in their wake.

We were all very busy with our painful work of transporting the dead and wounded from the streets of the compound, from the hooches and the bunkers—wherever we came upon them—then bandaging and treating them. Our emotions were necessarily deadened so that our legs would go where they must and our hands would do what needed to be done.

Therefore, when I came upon my friend, I became angry, wondering: *What right does he have to sit there all alone in the lobby with his head buried in his hands like that, sobbing like a baby?* The more I think about it, I think that is perhaps the reason the image remains stuck so in my mind. It's the sheer gall of the man to let himself go, to permit his whole body to be absorbed in this infantile act of weeping, blubbering as if he were only 10 years old. Or perhaps that is not an accurate statement, for I don't think I have ever seen a 10-year-old put his whole body into this behavior the way the man did that night—his shoulders rising and falling all in one piece, his tears soaking his palms and fingers so that they glistened in the artificial light—while out there in the darkness we were weaving in and out between the falling harbingers of death, wondering who among us would be next.

Then sometimes I think that my speechless, confused reaction, the awkward way I felt when I saw him, was due to my stunned (but unacknowledged) realization of the incongruity, the contrast, between his emotional upheaval and my own stolidity. For I knew so very well that I would not, could not, express my sorrow in such an open way.

* * *

Then there's Joe. It's curious that I recall his name, since he and I rarely talked. But there was something that always struck me about Joe—it was his calmness, the peace that seemed such an integral part of the man. I remember how he would sit on the end of his bunk for long intervals at a time gazing at photographs of his wife and children. He presented such an enigma to me. While the world around us seemed to be falling apart, Joe went about his days seemingly unperturbed.

One scene lingers more than the others and leaps out at me today across the years. It is one of Joe quietly turning the leaves of his Bible, which was small enough to be carried in his shirt pocket. It was not the fact that he owned the Bible or that I often saw him reading it that struck me so (many of the men read their Bibles and prayed—one doesn't have to consider the circumstances long to understand why this would be); rather, it was the peace of mind he so clearly possessed that impressed me. I noticed that he particularly displayed this sense of peace when reading his Bible. And Joe was such a nice guy! Although I didn't share his faith, I had to respect the calm disposition of the man. It always made me feel good to talk with him.

"Joe," I said to him one day, "nothing seems to rile you. While the rest of us are shaking in our boots, wondering if our number is going to be up next, or getting drunk at the club—doing just about anything in an effort to keep our sanity—you sit calmly reading your Bible, maintaining that steady, unworried demeanor. Why is that? Where does your peace of mind come from—this courage that you show?"

"Let me answer your question by telling you a story," he replied. "Can I do that? Do you know of the American Civil War general, Stonewall Jackson?"

"Of course."

"Well, the story goes that General Jackson was asked one day how it was that he could remain completely serene, steel-nerved, even in the very heat of battle, when the bullets were flying all about him as heavily as raindrops in a pouring storm. He answered that it was because he trusted in God. He knew that God was in control and would handle matters; therefore, such issues as his own death were of little concern to him. 'If all men trusted in God as I do,' he said, 'they would be equally brave.'

"And so it is with me. I place my trust in God. He will do what's best, and he knows what that is far better than I do. So why should I worry? And why should I be afraid?"

"Oh. Okay, I see. Well, that may work for you well enough. But me, I don't believe in God."

"Yes, so I've heard," said Joe. And I swear I saw a twinkle in the man's eye and a grin curling the ends of his lips. "I know," he repeated, looking intently at me, "and how is that going?"

The nerve of him, I thought to myself, *to make such a snide remark!* At his comment my temper flared, and I hastily turned and walked away, for I could not remain in the presence of such mockery; I was afraid I would show my anger and do something I shouldn't do. I wasn't always the nicest guy back then.

Yet in retrospect I realize that deep down I knew Joe wasn't mocking me. What angered me was that he challenged my assumptions, my fundamental worldview, which was so dear to me; it comprised the very core of who I was. His existence jeopardized the truth as I perceived it—the version of truth upon which I had staked my entire life. For he was a contradiction—neither weak of will nor mind, yet with a steadfast belief in God—and this combination did not fit my belief system. Suddenly I felt very insecure, as if I had been caught naked upon a stage. And I could not remain in the presence of such a person.

From that moment on I kept my distance from Joe. Yet, afterwards, whenever I walked by his bunk and caught him peacefully reading his Bible or one of his many devotional books, I was secretly envious. In fact, my envy was a secret even to me, for to acknowledge it would have been to crumble; my world would have toppled under the full weight of that realization.

BIBLE SELECTION

An oracle is within my heart
concerning the sinfulness of the wicked:
There is no fear of God before his eyes.
For in his own eyes he flatters himself
too much to detect or hate his sin.
The words of his mouth are wicked and deceitful;
he has ceased to be wise and to do good.
Even on his bed he plots evil;

he commits himself to a sinful course
and does not reject what is wrong (Ps. 36:1-4 NIV).

REFLECTION _____

At an unconscious level, something crucial to my salvation happened to my spirit in 1968 as I nightly ran for my life through the hail of mortar rounds. Until this war experience, I had fantastically assumed the following:

1. We humans are powerful and brilliant—our technology speaks for itself. After all, we have made it to the moon; just give us time and we will explore the galaxies.
2. We can and will cure all of our ills, both physical and social. We have found a cure for polio; soon we will rid our societies of war itself. Whatever problem exists today, just give us time, and we will solve it.

Today I realize that at a subliminal level I arrogantly made the following mental leap: we humans are worthy of deification, hence I will set myself up—that sample of humanity with which I am closest—as my very own god. In Vietnam, however, seeds of doubt were planted about the veracity of these statements, which eventually led me to death's front door, then ultimately to the true God—who most certainly wasn't me!

Yes, a thorn pierced my flesh and remained there, *a messenger of Satan, to torment me* (2 Cor. 12:7), for 18 long years. Due to my exorbitant self-pride, it took me that long to finally get the message and turn from self-adoration to pondering instead the majesty of God. That thorn in the flesh was two-fold:

1. A growing awareness of the vast limitations people have— the flaws that cut across the gamut of all humankind, leading to conflicts and wars; and
2. A realization, ever so subliminal, that in the long run humans cannot fix themselves. No real solution has ever been found for the primary human weakness: the tendency to look out for number one first and foremost, no matter how many others we must step over or kill in order to get our way.

Consequently, I have come to understand that the only true remedy for the shortcomings of mankind is a spiritual one.

Lord, forgive me for all of those years where my only allegiance was to myself. I realize now that I was being controlled by Satan, and that he was using me as his pawn. Dear God, thank you that my life was preserved and I did not die while in Satan's grip. Today your loving arms surround me, and I will rest in your undying love (Rom. 8:38-39).

In the precious name of Jesus Christ my Savior I pray. Amen.

CHAPTER ELEVEN

Bearing the World's Suffering

THREE THINGS OF NOTE occurred in my life while assigned as a reporter to the European edition of the U.S. armed forces newspaper, *Stars and Stripes*, from 1970 to 1974: my delightful son and daughter were born, I learned how to write, and I came face to face with my limitations in a way I never had before.

My babies, Chris and Jennifer, though they did not know it, held my heart in the palms of their hands. I was unworthy of the beautiful gift I was given when each came into my life; they have made my life worth living. I simply wish I had recognized the grandeur of the gift at the time and been a far better dad to them.

Assigned to the city desk of the *Stars and Stripes* in Darmstadt, West Germany, I fell head over heels in love with the written word. Initially I found the gruff and grizzly city editor Herb Scott quite intimidating. He repeatedly took a piece upon which I had slaved for hours and slashed it to bits so that when he handed it back to me it profusely bled red ink. He was bound and determined to make an effective journalist of me and, as I came to understand this, I relished his editing of my writing. I believe that his passion for teaching and my consequent respect for him turned me into a far better writer.

In 1971 he sent me, together with a photographer, on a 10-day excursion through Ethiopia to dig up feature material for the paper. My nose for news led us to a makeshift hospital outside Asmara where an English physician helicoptered in on occasion to provide pro bono medical care, the only medical treatment available for miles around.

There I watched in awe as people of a way of life utterly strange to me materialized like phantoms from the surrounding bush. Wearing the barest of threads, in appearance so weak it seemed a slight breeze might blow them over, they approached, forming a line at the entrance of the hospital. Listless youths and toothless, lame, emaciated adults—some cradling bloated, half-starved babies in their arms—stood patiently awaiting cursory medical care. It hit me that these were humans fundamentally like myself, except for the tragic misfortune of being born into a setting that destined them to a life of grinding poverty of a scope far greater than anything I had ever seen before.

It was the utter dullness of their eyes that froze me in my tracks, gripping me. *Is it despair I see in their eyes?* I wondered. No, it was rather a look of absolute resignation to whatever fate may hold in store, a complete submission to forces entirely beyond their control. As I had been when confronted with the plight of many Vietnamese, I was overcome with a deep desire to help these people, to remedy this wrong. But again, as in Vietnam, I was reminded of my impotence in the face of great need; I knew that by myself I could do nothing of lasting value for these people. It was this sense of powerlessness that ate at my gut.

My train of thought was abruptly broken as a young woman dashed from the waiting line. Then, leaning against a tree, a blanket clutched tightly in her arms, she softly wept. Impulsively I walked over to her and offered my assistance. Gasping back sobs, she gazed up directly into my eyes, her face glistening from the tears. Her eyes still fixed upon mine, she slowly unfolded the blanket, revealing a lifeless infant in her arms. Its small, bloated body sent shock waves through me. The look of pure desperation in that young mother's face still haunts me to this day.

Days later I stood on a bluff south of the Red Sea port of Masawa as a train of haggard men, women, and children in search of a better way of life wound their way laboriously across the difficult terrain below. As they drew nearer and their emaciated state became more evident, I studied the lost, tortured look in their eyes—and my heart went out to them!

Shaking my head sadly, I returned to the jeep, and the driver, my photographer, and I recommenced our convoluted trek up the mountainside to Masawa. Just 20 minutes later, we found our way ahead blocked by a company of men, women, and children looking uncannily like the troupe I had seen earlier. Observing them up close, the haunting looks on their gaunt and haggard faces burned holes into my heart. Yet it was the listless gaze in the eyes of the small children that touched me most of all.

The U.S. Army officer at the wheel approached them; a conversation ensued and minutes later he returned and said, "They won't let us through unless we give them some food." With that, he retrieved a large bundle from the rear of our vehicle. He presented it to them and the group parted, allowing us to pass. As we drove by I found myself hypnotically gazing into their faces. And for the first time in my life, I felt ashamed at having so much in the way of material possessions.

In retrospect, I find it intriguing that over the decades before I accepted Christ I felt an intense compassion for people in the abstract, yet by and large disliked people in the particular. So it was that I grieved for the desperate plight of the hurting masses of the globe even as I disliked virtually everyone I knew—most especially myself!

BIBLE SELECTION

"Peace I leave with you; my peace I give you. I do not give to you as the world gives. Do not let your hearts be troubled and do not be afraid.... [I]n me you may have peace. In this world you will have trouble. But take heart! I have overcome the world" (John 14:27; 16:33 NIV).

REFLECTION

For years I burned to help the poor and needy of the many countries I visited as I traversed the globe in the service of the armed forces; yet I felt utterly helpless to make a difference. My sole response was to observe rhetorically: *What can I, a solitary human being, do to help so many?* Consequently, I did nothing. An atheist, I was a common-sense, practical, matter-of-fact kind of person, with no understanding at all of the supernatural. Any hope I might muster was gauged strictly by the amount of strength I could detect within myself. As the years passed, I became more and more aware of how powerless I was in the face of enormous need. Oh, how I would have loved to find the strength to give sufficiently of myself!

"It is frequently said that to bear this world, we must become toughened, callous, hard," observed the Quaker missionary Thomas Kelly. "The sadness of the city-evils, the blighted lives we see, the injustices, the pains and tears! Without a protective covering of indifference, it seems rational to say, we cannot endure the world."[10]

How right Kelly is! One of my heaviest burdens for decades—from my Vietnam experience on—was a personal awareness of the misery of so much of the world's population. To rub shoulders with suffering people is a troubling experience for many of us; I bled for the people, and over time this burden was killing me.

However, when I accepted Christ, everything changed. I was no longer alone against all the evil and sorrow in the world; rather it was God and I together—a winning combination! *In all these things we are more than conquerors through him who loved us* (Rom. 8:37 NIV).

As Kelly wrote so eloquently:

> It is given to us to see the world's suffering, throughout, and bear it, Godlike, upon our shoulders, and suffer … and rejoice with all things and all people. There is a point of vision from which one can look through sorrow and pain and still see the face of the Eternal Lover.
>
> Overburdened men and women, blighted lives, slaveries in all their modern forms, nations and institutions in insane self-destruction, and little children hoping for warmth and love and opportunity [are all laid upon us]…. Pain inflicted on them becomes pain inflicted on ourselves. Were the experience not also an experience suffused with radiant peace and power and victory, as well as tragedy, it would be unbearable.[11]

Dear Lord, humbly I come before you today, thanking you for the grace to see your face in every person I encounter, especially those in desperate need. I am reminded that whatever I do for one of the least of these brothers of yours, I do for you. Relying on your strength and compassion manifested in me, reaching out to help meet the needs of hurting people, I find myself gratified and my faith strengthened. I learn that by serving as your ambassador of love, I keep my faith by giving it away; I feel you wrapping your arms about me, and I am overcome! Thank you, dear Jesus, for your sweet grace, which carries me through times of trouble.

In the precious name of Jesus Christ my Savior I pray. Amen.

CHAPTER TWELVE

The Man Who Made Me Feel Small

LOOKING BACK, I REALIZE that before the Lord came into my heart I was a small person in many ways. One of the best examples of this is the way I treated Gary Fisk.

I left the Air Force for the Navy in 1974. Gary, a thin 20-year-old man with delicate features, reported aboard the USS *Robison DDG-12* just a few months after I did. I had been recently promoted to work center supervisor and was feeling the power.

Gary had a problem with getting up on time in the morning. I was feeling my oats, and I rode him hard. People who know me now tell me they can't imagine me yelling at a subordinate, but before the Lord softened me, I yelled often. I yelled at my wife, I yelled at my children, and I yelled at Gary. Gary's reaction, however, was to shrink into a kind of shell. This irritated me to no end; it exasperated me.

Every fourth day my section was scheduled for duty, and I would arrive on station promptly at 6:30 a.m. The scene that followed was as predictable as the sunrise. I would pace the deck, checking my watch, complaining to the others in my section about Gary's habitual tardiness. As we broke up, going to our various assignments, Gary would inevitably come dragging up the ladder, unshaven, hair in disarray, uniform wrinkled. In my mind's eye, I can still see him striding toward me, head lowered, his eyes avoiding mine, awaiting the inevitable. I most certainly did not disappoint him but jumped into him with both feet, calling him every bad name in the book. As I screamed at him, he cowered more and more, withdrawing further and further into himself.

Today I wonder: if I had sincerely given him an ear, and, patiently and impartially, heard him out, perhaps Gary would have opened up and shared from his heart, providing me an insight, an understanding of the man inside. As it was, he appeared terrified of me; and, consequently (although I was completely oblivious of it at the time), I despised myself. Yes, the more I offended Gary, the more I offended myself. And, although I wrote him up for tardiness again and again, his bad habits did not cease.

A few weeks later, on the first leg of a Western Pacific cruise, we pulled into Pearl Harbor on a Friday for a weekend of refueling and restocking. Saturday morning our section had the duty; but when the day dawned—no Gary. Asking around, I found that he and a friend went into the city the afternoon before and hadn't made it back. I was standing topside when I spotted him finally straggling aboard, looking the worse for the wear. I was fierce. Dashing down the ladder, I stood waiting until he crossed the quarterdeck. Noticing me, he quickly ducked his head and glanced away.

I must have been red-faced, for the wrath was building in me to the point of losing control. There in front of all the quarterdeck personnel, I dressed Gary down, calling him a dirty dog and every other colorful term that came to mind. It was so bad that afterwards an officer who witnessed the scene pulled me aside and voiced his contempt for my leadership style. He dressed *me* down. This made me even madder, and I went gunning for Gary.

Today I know that without God in your heart displaying his curative love, you disdain both yourself and others. And, oh, how I despised Gary at that moment. I was embarrassed, and I blamed my own troubles on him. And I knew a way to get even.

Gary had recently been promoted to petty officer third class, and on this particular write-up for unauthorized absence, I criticized his performance as a new noncommissioned officer—detailing all his infractions, particularly his chronic tardiness. I described him as incorrigible and recommended he be brought to captain's mast and reduced to the rank of seaman. I omitted the fact that he was an excellent technician and had good interpersonal skills. This especially irritated me, for I couldn't understand why others liked him, could get inside his shell, but I could not. I knew him not at all.

Captain's mast was held on the fantail on a sunny morning three days later while dolphins leaped alongside the ship as we carved the placid waters on our way west. As I approached the group of men standing in formal procession for the grave event, Gary emerged from below decks, and our paths briefly crossed. His eyes met mine for what seemed like the first time ever, and the chilly look he cast still stings across 30 years. It was a bitter, accusative glare which cut me to the quick. The stare seemed so out of character for the man that it stopped me dead in my tracks—this was not the Gary I had assumed him to be. I had been so sure of myself, but now I felt disoriented and befuddled.

When our names were called, we stepped smartly forward. Gary and I stood side by side as the captain read the charges. He asked me a few questions then addressed Gary, who said nothing in his own defense. As the captain spoke the solemn words that divested him of his single stripe, my gut felt suddenly very empty; the sense of satisfaction I thought would be forthcoming was disappointingly absent. I glanced at Gary. The look on his face was one of grim disappointment and deep sadness. For the first time I felt a twinge of guilt and, at some level, I realized I was wrong.

Following the captain's mast, I was strangely overcome with a compulsion to speak with Gary, though I wasn't sure what I wished to say to him. Looking back, I can see I was trying to find a way to assuage my guilt—the uneasiness I was now feeling was troubling me immensely. Consequently, I went looking for Gary and finally found him chatting with some friends on the fo'c'sle. As I approached, I noticed the bare outline on his sleeve marking where his stripe had been, and I felt a sadness I couldn't explain, a sudden feeling of shame.

Spotting me from the corner of one eye, he abruptly turned, walking rapidly away. I waved and called out to him, but he ignored me, picking up his stride. I felt sadly empty and impotent for I knew Gary wasn't going to give me the opportunity to speak with him. The uneasiness I felt was driving me crazy.

Over the days that followed, Gary continued to behave coldly toward me. He was now refusing to respond when I addressed him directly. A week after the demotion, we pulled into a South Seas island port. Much of the crew was tired from hard work the day before and I was assigned as officer of the deck for the 4 a.m. watch. Gary was assigned as messenger of the watch under my supervision. When he did not report on time for duty—as had happened so many times before—I went looking for him.

Approaching his rack in the near total darkness of the compartment below deck, I heard issuing from it mysterious, soft, sobbing sounds. When I realized it was Gary, I couldn't believe my ears. "Fisk! Fisk! You're 15 minutes late for your watch! When will you ever learn? Get up, you lazy _____!"

The cruel words that escaped my lips were too malicious and cutting to repeat, and I grieve that I ever said them, for I can never take them back. To my chagrin, despite my continuous yelling, Gary appeared oblivious of my presence. He did not respond, but remained in his rack, continuing to cry like a small child. Then a soft, eerie voice emanated from him: "Go away! Go away!"

"Gary, get up, you _____!" But he said no more, though the cries persisted. I finally gave up and was headed back to the quarterdeck, preparing to write him up once again, when another seaman approached. Startled, I asked, "What are you doing up, Jones? You're not on duty." Seaman Bill Jones explained how he had been tapped to pull Gary's watch. He told me what he thought everyone knew—that Gary had received a radio message the day before informing him that his father had died suddenly. At 6:30 a.m., a chopper was scheduled to pick him up and fly him out to a carrier where he would catch a plane back home.

It was as if I had been hit between the eyes with a brick. I was stunned! Now it all made sense—the weeping, the words which issued from him: "Go away! Go away!" I felt as small as a man could possibly feel.

Watching a while later by early morning light as Gary ascended by way of a cable to a helicopter hovering above the ship was as close to a religious experience as this atheist had ever come. I remembered the accusing look he gave me prior to the captain's mast and felt once more that I had been weighed in the scales and come up wanting. I was certain I was going to melt into the deck beneath my feet. I was a lonely, cowering man, lost against the vastness of the sea.

I never saw Gary again. We had expected him to return, to join up with the ship at another port. But something transpired that changed all that. I was disappointed, hoping against all hope (I realize today) to somehow make amends. Instead, God saw fit to leave this hole inside of me. This incident, like so many others, was a burden I was to lay down years later at the foot of the cross of Jesus Christ.

BIBLE SELECTION

Love is patient, love is kind. It does not envy, it does not boast, it is not proud. It is not rude, it is not self-seeking, it is not easily angered, it keeps no record of wrongs. Love does not delight in evil but rejoices with the truth. It always protects, always trusts, always hopes, always perseveres. Love never fails…. And now these three remain: faith, hope and love. But the greatest of these is love (1 Cor. 13:4-8, 13 NIV).

REFLECTION_____

The more I offended Gary, the more I offended myself. This observation from my memory is lodged deep within my mind and grieves me greatly today—it eats at me. I keep asking myself: *If my actions toward Gary offended me so, why did I continue in them? If I recognized the error of my behavior, why didn't I stop?* In reflecting upon the matter, I see these elements at work:

1. I did not like myself; in fact, I somewhat hated myself. This dislike of myself was part and parcel of the reason I disliked others.
2. At that time in my life, I was deeply suspicious of others, of their motives. I believe this was evident in my behavior toward them. I didn't really trust myself, so how could I trust others?
3. Because I disliked myself (and others) so, I felt compelled to punish myself as well as to strike out at other people; it was a compulsion over which I had no control. And to top it off, I was not even aware of it. In punishing myself I felt (subliminally) that I was giving myself what I deserved. Thus I continued in my self-destructive behavior even as I failed to understand it.
4. These characteristics were there preeminently because I did not believe in God. Because of my atheism, I deferred to myself alone as my sole authority and source of power. Aware of my vast limitations, I hated myself for letting myself (and the significant others in my life) down again and again.

I have come to see that our love of God is the basis—the driving force—of our love for self and others. The commandments our Lord named as the greatest are about love of God, other people, and ourselves. They are all integrally related and hold the secret of true compassion. The reason I was so miserable is because these were not a part of my life, my mindset, at the time I knew Gary.

I pray, dear Lord, that I will treat the people I encounter daily in ways pleasing to you; that I will display your tender patience with them; that I will take the time to listen to them, to hear them out, and to behave lovingly toward them. May they see Christ in me! I know that if I obey your greatest commandment—to humbly love you with all my heart and mind and soul—then you, dear Lord, will guide me—my thoughts, my words, my actions. *He leads the humble in what is right, teaching them his way. The Lord leads with unfailing love and faithfulness all those who keep his covenant and obey his decrees. For the honor of your name, O Lord, forgive my many, many sins. Who are those who fear the Lord? He will show them the path they should choose* (Ps. 25:9-12 NLT).

In the precious name of Jesus Christ my Savior I pray. Amen.

CHAPTER THIRTEEN

The Wretchedness of Ambivalence

AS A YOUNG ADULT, my bigotry and arrogance ruled me just as much as they had when I was a boy. Nevertheless, I honestly considered myself enlightened. After all, hadn't I outgrown the limitations of my upbringing as early as age 14 when, after a careful consideration of all the evidence, I had concluded that there was no God and set myself up as judge and jury of everyone around me? Couldn't I quote Keats and Shelley and Faulkner and Goethe? Didn't that make me enlightened?

With such an irrational, boastful attitude toward the world, it was no wonder that I was confused by the mixed feelings aroused within me when I first met and talked with Petty Officer Third Class Jimmy Sparks. He was a short, stocky, quiet young man from Mississippi who rarely spoke in my presence. When he did, his sentences were always curt and to the point, which reinforced my gut feeling that he, being black, was necessarily of inferior intelligence. I believed this despite much evidence to the contrary, for I had read the novels of James Baldwin, the poetry of Langston Hughes, and the sermons of Martin Luther King Jr. I had been moved by the acting of Sidney Poitier. At an intellectual level, I was fully aware that racial prejudice was both irrational and morally wrong. Yet the boundaries of my mental world were so contrived that I could not see clearly enough, nor far enough, to recognize the truth of my own shortcomings.

A naval destroyer like the USS *Robison* is a relatively small vessel; consequently, everyone aboard knows everyone else's habits. When I noticed that Sparks typically hung out with the few other African-American sailors on board, I concluded that this was evidence of racial prejudice on his part, that he considered himself superior to white men, that he was "uppity." (The contradiction evidenced by the fact that I personally socialized only with white sailors blew right past me.) Today I realize that my thinking at the time went something like this: *Of course he hangs with his own kind. African-*

Americans would be uncomfortable with people of our superior intelligence and education. They need their own rogue language and inferior music and crass conversation in order to feel at ease. Seeing Sparks laughing and joking with the other black men in the mess hall, yet behaving moodily (or so it seemed) around me, deeply infuriated me and only reinforced my bigoted notions about him.

Sparks refused at all times to meet my glance. I know today that this aspect of his behavior was likely cultural; it was a learned behavior. When I addressed him, he invariably dropped his eyes, and this annoyed me to no end. *He's got something to hide, or he greatly resents me,* I concluded. *Why else won't he look me in the eye?*

Consequently, I found Sparks' presence in my work center increasingly disconcerting, and I set out to punish him for daring to masquerade as a competent technician, to assume he could do the work of a white man (while all the time I was not consciously aware of this, my true motive). We all made occasional errors in our work; we all forgot things from time to time. But it was Sparks whom I wrote up time and time again for poor performance and insubordination. It never occurred to me to encourage him (as I occasionally did my white subordinates). I never considered that I might not be objectively assessing his work performance; in fact, had you questioned me at the time, I would have insisted that I was very objective. I didn't allow for the possibility that his behavior might be due directly to my own poor leadership. I certainly never attempted to see the world (or myself) through his eyes. (If it had even occurred to me to do so, I don't believe I would have known how to begin.) Rather, arrogantly and wrongly, I passed judgment on him based solely on my own emotions and prejudices. Therefore Sparks had to be taught a lesson! That was my job! I was most assuredly doing the right thing!

It pains me in retrospect to imagine how extremely frustrating it must have been for him to report to work each day, attempting to do his job, with this pigheaded redneck (me) lording over him, prejudging him, utterly refusing to give him a fair hearing, an honest opportunity to express what was really going on with him. Now that I think about it, it was probably this insurmountable barrier that drove Sparks to ultimately take the recourse he did.

From the moment he reported to my work center, the writing was on the wall that I would, in time, bring charges of insubordination. These eventually made their way up the chain of command to the captain; Sparks and I were given a date and time to report to the commanding officer for non-judicial punishment to be handed down.

In the days leading up to the captain's mast, I felt very uncomfortable when passing Sparks in a passageway or glancing at him across the deck; he glared at me with an accusing, angry stare. Gone was the old behavior of dropping his eyes in my presence, rather his eyes now openly conveyed hate and his lips formed a sneer. There was no misunderstanding his feelings.

At last, we both stood before the captain in his stateroom and I heard him levy the punishment: For insubordination, i.e., for ignoring my verbal commands on multiple occasions, Petty Officer Third Class Jimmy Sparks was stripped of his petty officer rank. He was once again Seaman Sparks. I was on cloud nine, feeling gratified and reassured of the correctness of my actions. I had helped make the world a little better, putting things back the way they should be. However, I noticed Sparks' jaw muscles tighten as the punishment was being meted out. And as I left the captain's stateroom, from the corner of one eye I spotted Sparks glaring at me; he was furious. A bolt of fear shot through me. *This is not the way it should be,* I thought to myself (always at a subliminal level). *He should be thanking me for helping set things right. It's wrong for a black man to be an electronics technician. He should have chosen one of the less demanding roles, one that doesn't require as much in the way of smarts, one he perhaps could handle.*

A half hour later, as I was stepping into the ship's aft head, the lights abruptly went out. One second I was standing, the next lying on my back on the floor, peering up through a fog at Sparks, standing, glaring downward at me. Struggling to deduce what had occurred, I became suddenly aware of a severe head pain that wouldn't stop. I lifted a hand to my bruised head as the truth abruptly dawned on me. "Sparks, you slugged me! I'll get you for this! I'll just write you up again! You haven't achieved a thing! This was stupid of you." But Sparks' seething chest and great angry snarl were fixed in place; he remained unfazed by my threats. Abruptly, he turned and left.

A week later we were back in front of the captain. Seaman Sparks stolidly stared directly ahead, refusing to even acknowledge that I was present. As the captain solemnly ordered his reduction by one more pay grade to the rank of seaman apprentice, Sparks remained calm, to all appearances unmoved. This time, however, I was completely devoid of any feelings of gratification; rather, a sense of profound failure fell over me, for deep down I realized I was doing something seriously wrong.

I was now haunted by the incensed look I had seen in Sparks' face as he stared down at me where I lay outstretched on the floor of the head. This image would haunt me for the rest of my life. For at that moment I finally grasped just how hurt and angry he was and I recognized the possibility that something was very awry with my version of the world.

BIBLE SELECTION

"Why do you look at the speck of sawdust in your brother's eyes and pay no attention to the plank in your own eye? How can you say to your brother, 'Let me take the speck out of your eye,' when all the time there is a plank in your own eye? You hypocrite, first take the plank out of your own eye, and then you will see clearly to remove the speck from your brother's eye" (Matt. 7:3-5 NIV).

REFLECTION

One of the constancies of hypocrisy is that the hypocrite is never aware of his or her condition—in fact, at the very moment one becomes aware, the hypocrisy begins to subside. Therefore, in order to reach up to remove the speck of sawdust from my own eye, I must first become aware it is there. An essential element of any recovery program worth its salt is that the recovering person must first of all recognize the problem and the consequent need to change.

I was absolutely certain I was no bigot; yet there I was passing judgment on Jimmy Sparks, convinced that he was a racist since he appeared to prefer the company of other African-Americans. The fact that people with common cultural interests may prefer one another's company and that this may have been the reason for Sparks' choice never occurred to me. I never once attempted to analyze why I tended to be nervous and uncomfortable in the company of African-Americans, or wondered why it was that their race was the first thing I noticed about them. I had thick blinders on, but at the same time was too blind to see them. I just assumed that I was the objective one, yet the only justification for my assumption was my need to believe I was right, born of my own arrogance.

I have since learned that there are at least two compartments to our minds:

1. The superficial, intellectualizing compartment, where we consciously come to some conclusion or another; and
2. The gut level compartment, the place within us where we really live, where our biases lay securely rooted within our subconscious. To become fully aware of the contents of this compartment—so that we can look at the problem and do something about it—requires interaction with the Holy Spirit. Our mental health is contingent upon this.

As an atheist, I couldn't pray at the time the verses I often do today: *Search me, O God, and know my heart; test me and know my anxious thoughts. See if there is any offensive way in me, and lead me in the way everlasting* (Ps. 139:23-24 NIV).

It was only after I accepted Christ in midlife and began seriously, prayerfully pondering Christ's teachings that, by degrees, I became aware of my deeply entrenched prejudices, the product of my upbringing. As I permitted Christ more and more to examine my heart and teach me his ways, I eventually saw how far and deep the tentacles of racial prejudice were rooted within me. Just as the bulk of an iceberg is hidden beneath the surface of the sea, so the substance of the racial bias ingrained within me laid beyond the scope of my consciousness and ruled me from an insensitive netherworld. As Christ made me increasingly aware of this, I was able to receive and apply the remedy, the effectual remedy of his curative love.

I wish to speak to those of you readers who may be struggling with the issue of prejudice of any kind. I have learned through life experience that we will always be blind to this tendency until we back up and seriously study how Christ lived his life. Since his name is Love (1 John 4:16), he is a God of unconditional love, therefore there are none whom he does not love. Seeing deep into the heart of each person, Christ recognizes no labels. He has always loved us, despite any label that others may have placed on us, or that we may even have placed upon ourselves. *While we were still sinners, Christ died for us* (Rom. 5:8 NIV).

Since Christ has always loved each of us deeply, despite our labels, we must learn to see others in the same way: label-free. And this can only be achieved through the perfect love of Christ in us (Matt. 5:48), which he tells us to display. This is the only perfection to which God calls us while we are at home in this body. He truly expects us to love everyone, even our enemies, just as he does (Matt. 5:44).

God sees no labels and neither must we!

Dear Lord, please search me and know my heart. See if there is any offensive way in me and lead me in the way everlasting. I am so sorry that I hurt Jimmy Sparks so many years ago. Looking back at the confusion and anger and resentment—much of it born of prejudice—that dominated my life at the time, I feel I should don sackcloth and ashes, sit in a corner, and pray a long prayer of deepest contrition to you, my God.

I pray that I will demonstrate and project a loving attitude today. May your loving heart be evident in my behavior, dear Lord.

In the precious name of Jesus Christ my Savior I pray. Amen.

CHAPTER FOURTEEN

The Persistent Proselytizer

WALTER MULLINS HAD NO right to exist.

His spit-shined shoes, perfectly creased shirt, and confident demeanor were an insult to me. An egoist when I was in the Navy, I viewed everything only as it related to myself. From the moment Walter reported aboard ship—I was there when he first strode across the bow, sea bag arrogantly slung across one shoulder, hat cocked on the back of his head—he bugged me; I took his walk for a swagger and his smile for a sneer. I think my feelings were a response to that self-satisfied look he fixed on me, as if he were judging me somehow, sizing me up to be something small.

You see, Walter Mullins was an evangelical Christian. He made absolutely no secret of his faith. He challenged me early on about my self-proclaimed atheism, and we got into it more than once.

The reason I state in such stark terms that Walter had no right to exist is because there was absolutely no place for someone like him in my belief system. In my concrete worldview, religious people—particularly Christians—were uneducated, uncouth simpletons, so in need of a crutch that they invented one and called it God. Walter was one of the few people I had met who flatly did not fit that stereotype. I found this exasperating.

I recall one late evening, when making my rounds, I opened the hatch to the missile fire control radar room to find him and a few others sitting on the floor in a circle, each with a Bible in hand. At first I didn't grasp what was happening. When it dawned on me, I was completely thrown. "You guys really do get into this nonsense, don't you!" I snapped.

Without batting an eyelash, Walter replied, "Sit down and join us, Glen. We'll catch you up. We'd love to have you; wouldn't we, guys?" They all murmured in the affirmative.

"You've got to be kidding me!" I snorted, storming out of the compartment.

The next day I found a note on my rack—a folded piece of paper upon which was scribbled a Scripture verse, *"Be still, and know that I am God"* (Ps. 46:10 NIV), with a comment, "A wise person would ponder this." (I find it eerie that I recall this across so many years. Perhaps not coincidentally, this same verse played a significant role in me coming to Christ a decade later.) At the time, I simply snickered, arrogantly wadded it up, and tossed it into the trash.

But as the notes continued coming, I became annoyed, and finally angry. I scowled and stormed about ship, questioning everyone I met: "Who is putting these notes on my rack?" No one owned up. But I suspected it was Walter.

Meanwhile, Walter's reputation grew; he became more and more respected for his competence and leadership skills by both the officers and his peers. One day, when I had finally had enough, I happened upon him up on the fo'c'sle talking with a couple of his Christian cohorts. Standing nose to nose with Walter, my face flushed with anger, I waved a note in front of his face and demanded, "Are you putting these on my rack?"

He smiled calmly back at me. He was, as always, cleanly shaven, his hair perfect in every detail. Greatly irritated, I waved the note wildly, shouting myself hoarse above the ocean roar.

"Glen, why does this trouble you so much?" he asked, shouting back. Then, for the first time, I saw something in his face that upset me even more. I could read it in his eyes: Walter sincerely cared about me. He was really deeply concerned. And that disturbed me most of all. He had no right to care!

Wiping the salt water from my face, I snapped, "Don't you go pitying me, you, you ... I don't need your compassion. Leave me alone!" Oblivious of the small crowd that had gathered around, I lost control, my anger and resentment taking over. "I don't need your God! And I don't need you!"

I was so furious, I envisioned myself slapping and choking the man. Today I recognize that my worse fears were being realized; my vision of the world was shattering into fragments. Deep within me my heart was screaming: *This man defies everything I have come to believe! He can't be real!*

Shortly afterwards, the notes ceased. Still, every time I encountered Walter, the anger seethed within me. I could not understand at the time why he disturbed me so much. This was the rule with my emotional life in those days: I had little say in my feelings; I was entirely reactive. Why I felt such antipathy toward Walter, I hadn't a clue.

BIBLE SELECTION _____

For Christ's love compels us, because we are convinced that one died for all, and therefore all died. And he died for all, that those who live should no longer live for themselves but for him who died for them and was raised again.

So from now on we regard no one from a worldly point of view. Though we once regarded Christ in this way, we do so no longer. Therefore, if anyone is in Christ, he is a new creation; the old has gone, the new has come! All this is from God, who reconciled us to himself through Christ and gave us the ministry of reconciliation: that God was reconciling the world to himself in Christ, not counting men's sins against them. And he has committed to us the message of reconciliation. We are therefore Christ's ambassadors, as though God were making his appeal through us. We implore you on Christ's behalf: Be reconciled to God (2 Cor. 5:14-20 NIV).

REFLECTION _____

It's intriguing how Walter's image has haunted me through the decades. I met him in my late 20s—today I am almost 60—yet I see his face as clearly as if it were yesterday. The look of sincerity I saw on Walter's face when I confronted him on the fo'c'sle sent shock waves through me that reverberated down the years to this moment. I saw a calm compassion in the man's eyes like that I'm sure was in the eyes of the Lord Jesus when he came face to face with rebellious egos.

We read in Mark 5:6-7 how a demon-possessed man, when he saw Jesus, *fell on his knees in front of him. He shouted at the top of his voice, "What do you want with me, Jesus, Son of the Most High God? Swear to God that you won't torture me!"* When this man saw Jesus, he knew he was confronted with God himself, and he pleaded not to be tortured. I know I saw in Walter that day something of Christ, and I was similarly threatened. It was like I had been found out, that the lie by which I lived my life had been revealed for what it was. But I wasn't going to give up that easily. Unlike the demon-possessed man, when confronted by the Truth in human form, I was not going to go down without a fight; rather, my ego, my self-reliance, my emotional crutch shouted silently from deep within me: *I am the king of the universe, the god in my own life. I will call the shots, I and no other!* These words, translated into the language of the moment were: "I don't need your God! And I don't need you!"

The lie within me was suffocating because it found itself face to face with Christ in Walter Mullins, and it was determined to fight back.

I wish to address everyone who actively witnesses for Christ: Don't give up. In retrospect I know that from that time forward, within the deepest recesses of my being lay the realization that my view of reality was deeply flawed. The spirit of Christ in Walter was recognized for what it was. It took 10 years, but I eventually came around. The seed we plant in those to whom we witness may not be evident at the time, but it can make all the difference later on.

Dear Lord, thank you sending Walter my way. Thank you for communicating through him the love and care you have for me. Walter saw me with the eyes of God, saw through my arrogant façade to what I really was—a poor, insecure fool attempting vainly to hold on to a shallow, silly myth that had no merit at all. He knew I would remain miserable until I accepted the Truth that is you, Lord.

I pray that I may be a light to others, as Walter was for me. He planted a seed that eventually produced fruit. Like Walter, I pray that I will always be ready to give the reason for the hope I have in Christ (1 Pet. 3:15).

In the precious name of Jesus Christ my Savior I pray. Amen.

CHAPTER FIFTEEN

The Bottoming Out of Despair

"KA-WHUMP! KA-WHUMP!"

I sat up abruptly in bed and glanced disconcertingly about the room. *Are those mortar rounds?* I wondered. Desperately attempting to discern reality, I evaluated my circumstances. Then it hit me: this was one more dream—another in a series of nightmares that never ceased.

Eighteen years had elapsed since I served in the war, yet repeatedly, unwittingly, I traveled back there in my mind: the frantic rush from hooch to bunker, attempting absurdly to dodge incoming shells; then hunkering, shuddering amongst my comrades as the rounds slam the earth; next, madly racing through the darkness to speed the ambulance down the streets of the compound, seeking out fallen friends; and finally, tenderly embracing the wounded as I wrap bandages in place. Tragically, a grip falters, a friend's hand goes limp, and my rage mounts against an unseen enemy.

Despairingly, I watch the mound of corpses grow. As my guilt feelings intensify, I bury them forcibly, as if they, too, were mere dead things. I refuse to acknowledge them, for there is no time to mourn—the demands of those still living require my full attention. Yet a deep sense of loss still lingers all these years later.

What is human life anyway? I ask myself. *Is a man no more than a fly on the wall? Or a dead dog whose carcass we dump into a roadside ditch? Must I lose Bill also before I'm through mourning Charlie? And must I lose Steve before I've had time to mourn Bill? Oh, scythe-bearer, have you no respect at all for human life?*

An atheist, unlike most who served with me in Vietnam, my dog tags read: No Religious Preference. I recognized no God to whom I might turn, therefore my despair continued to mount.

* * *

As my 13-year-old daughter struggled against the pulls of the world, and the needs of my 14-year-old son blazed out to me from across the room, I remained focused upon myself. As my wife sought reassurance and support in her efforts to reach them, I selfishly failed her as well. For there was a fire inside my heart that burned and burned, an open wound that I could not heal—that was my priority. It sapped all my strength, all my intense energy.

I vividly remember the day I made a conscious decision to no longer respond to my wife's continual appeals. Coiled up facing the back of the sofa, numbed by the pain pills the doctor prescribed for my chronic migraine headaches, I enwrapped myself in an invisible cocoon and would not respond when my wife called out to me. She stood only a foot away, screaming with all her might. I do not remember her words, but the message in her voice was clear: Help me! Help me! It was a cry of pure despair issuing from deep within her. I could summon no strength with which to come to her aid. I refused to move, to turn and face her. The greater the anguish in her cries, the more tightly I coiled up my body, until my knees nearly touched my chin.

On countless occasions the war of words so filled the house that I felt as if my chest were impaled with flaming arrows. I was so ill that the anguish of this daily assault strangely brought me a morbid sense of sanctimoniousness; I overtly blamed everyone but myself. I regularly flung myself out the door and down the block to a favorite solitary spot behind a Safeway store, where for hours I sat and nursed my self-pity, wondering how I was ever going to escape from the addictive demons of existential despair. I saw no exit.

In our family therapy sessions, the doctor implored me to reach deep within myself and summon the strength to follow her recommendations, but I could find no strength. In vain she pleaded, yet I could not produce. Eventually a death wish set in.

I remember like yesterday the excitement I felt when the thought first came over me—though, in retrospect, it seems quite eerie. I felt like a child in a candy store, realizing for the first time that I could pocket some when no one was looking, or like the way I felt at age six when I rose on Christmas morning before the others and snuck out of my bedroom to open the gifts there for me beneath the Christmas tree. For, you see, in considering suicide I was encroaching upon forbidden terrain. Although dangerous, the lure was so seductive that I felt I must somehow make the move.

Just a dozen or so of these pills, I thought, *taken with a glass of water, and I will slip away into a quiet, comfortable place where I can finally rest. It will be like taking a long overdue nap, one from which I will never awaken.* Few things are as seductive as sleep. How many times have we groggily fumbled for the alarm

clock to turn it off so we could slip back into slumber? *Death must be like that,*
I thought. *No more pain! No more impossible demands! No more despair washing
over me until, like a martyr burned alive at the stake, I howl out in a maddening
cry of anguish that exhausts every atom of my being, yet brings no relief. The
flames fail to annihilate me—oh, how I wish they would!—they merely continue
to engulf me in indescribable pain!*

For three long days I nursed my secret suicide plan—a way out of the misery
of the world. As the thrill of that Christmas long ago revisited me hourly, I lifted
the bottle of little yellow pills, unscrewed the cap, and poured them one by one
into my palm. *Oh, how I love the way they numb me! And if I took a dozen, they would
lull me off into a place of forgetfulness where I would feel no more pain.*

Then the moment arrived. I remember sitting in my office at the 32nd
Street Naval Station, holding the bottle before me with both hands, when
the compulsion to finally carry out my secret plan washed over me like a
warm sea wave on a sandy beach. My heart beat faster and faster, loudly
throbbing in my chest. I was like a child pondering his first roller coaster
ride, watching the cars speeding their serpentine way into the sky, listening
to the passengers scream from the thrill of the ride. Now it was my turn, my
turn! My hands trembled with excitement as I unscrewed the cap and poured
the contents into my palm once more, then made my way to the sink for a
glass of water. Then, suddenly, I froze in my tracks. From somewhere deep
within me arose a voice that had long been silent, a part of myself I did not
recognize at first, which shouted out: *I don't want to die!*

Now where did that come from? I wondered. *Remember: to live is only pain!*
And the compulsion returned in full force, the drive to kill myself that would
not be stilled! Moving quickly, before the voice of preservation could win
out, I poured the glass of water. Then, holding the full glass in my hand,
again I froze. *I don't want to die!* howled out the voice. I hastily put down the
glass, replaced the pills in their container and shoved it into my pocket, then
abruptly thrust myself out the door and down the street.

As I headed across the compound to where my car was parked, I passed
the base dispensary as I did every day. But on this particular day, I stopped
just outside the building. It was as if I was trapped within a confined space
between two opposing and equally strong obsessions—one: to kill myself;
the other: to stay alive. And I was terrified of the consequences of either.
Suddenly, I hit upon a third alternative, another possible avenue, though I
had no idea what its outcome might be.

I entered the dispensary. Shortly afterwards I was called into the doctor's office and I told him of my mental tug of war. As I explained my suicide plan, a look of urgency appeared upon his face. Moments later, an ambulance was speeding me across town to Balboa Naval Hospital.

BIBLE SELECTION

We do not want you to be uninformed, brothers, about the hardships we suffered in the province of Asia. We were under great pressure, far beyond our ability to endure, so that we despaired even of life. Indeed, in our hearts we felt the sentence of death. But this happened that we might not rely on ourselves but on God, who raises the dead (2 Cor. 1:8-9 NIV).

REFLECTION

To die or not to die? To live or not to live? "When there is no answer for death," wrote Ravi Zacharias, "despair inevitably invades life."[12] Without a belief in Heaven, we seek heaven in this world; when heaven fails to materialize and instead we find ourselves in a living hell, we fall into despair. That was my dilemma.

And since there is also no belief in an afterlife, death for the atheist is seen simply as a long, deep, dreamless sleep from which he will never emerge. If life for such a one is only pain, then death becomes the avenue by which to escape from that pain! And so I believed.

In my atheistic mindset, I saw no God, no Heaven, no Hell; I simply wanted to live, yet I was bound by the increasing realization that I could not even live with myself. Therefore I began to consider death, which to me at the time was but the cessation of the pain of living—a horrific state of being from which I sought relief.

Looking back, I see that I was entirely calling the shots—playing God in my life. With no divine resources at my disposal, I had finally exhausted all recourses; I had arrived at the end of myself. I was completely, utterly lost. Living for me had become hell.

E. Stanley Jones hit on the core of the problem:

> We who decided we would not live with God, find that we
> cannot live with ourselves. A sinner is one who is literally
> a problem to himself. The hell which modern man banished
> from the universe by politely putting it out at the door, has
> now come back through the window in the form of neuroses,
> fears, inhibitions, inner conflicts, [and] guilts.[13]

Neuroses, fears, inhibitions, inner conflicts, guilt—I suffered from all of these, and they were driving me mad! Today I vividly recall the pain I felt. How close I came! It is a wonder that I escaped!

Dear God, thank you for forgiving me for choosing to live so long without you. How lost I was! How selfish I was! How foolish I was! Yet when I eventually did turn to you and repent of my sins, you were promptly there for me; you forgave me the guilt of my sins and set me free! I am so blessed to have such a patient, forgiving God who loves me despite all the wrongs I have done. I will be forever grateful!

In the precious name of Jesus Christ my Savior I pray. Amen.

CHAPTER SIXTEEN

Awash in a Sea of Guilt

SOON I WAS STANDING at the counter of the Balboa Naval Hospital sixth floor "psych ward," howling in protest as the staff confiscated my pain medication. "Those are prescribed!" I shouted at them. "You have no right to take them!"

"This is your *new* doctor's orders," I was told bluntly as they took not only my pills but also my belt, showed me a locker where I could store a few select personal items, then provided me with a pair of loose-fitting pajamas.

Finally realizing my cries were to no avail, I settled into a straight-back chair. In time I became aware that I was staring fixedly down at my hands, my head throbbing like a locomotive. Slowly turning my hands over and over in my lap, I examined them in minute detail, the thick dark hair on the back and the creases of the palms, which reminded me of a map of a hinterland. Unexplainably, my eyes were transfixed on them. I wanted to do nothing more for all the rest of my life but sit still, quietly staring down at my hands.

I was awash in a sea of guilt, and the world seemed a featureless gray all about me. The dialogue and motions of others in the room seemed to have nothing at all to do with me. I had found a posture, an activity of sorts, which suited me. I reached the conclusion that if I sat in this fashion for hour upon hour, intensely nursing my personal anguish, then my misery would somehow become tolerable.

From out of nowhere came a woman's commanding voice. Glancing up, I noticed she was standing toe to toe with me, frowning down disapprovingly. In one hand she held a broom.

"Here! Sweep the floor!" she ordered. I ignored her, staring back down at my hands. She repeated, "I said, 'Sweep the floor!'" I did not respond. "Sweep this floor!" she said again firmly.

I glanced up, annoyed, screaming silently within myself: *How dare she spoil my moments of morbid depression? Intrude upon my fantasy world of petty selfishness? What gives her the right?* I sneered. "No!" I shouted back. "No! I don't feel well! I'm sick! They took away my headache pain pills and won't give them back!"

"I'll say it just one more time: Get up!"

I felt belittled, offended. Like a child forced against his will to do his household chores, I angrily stood up, stomping my feet in the process. With exaggerated gestures, I grabbed the broom and commenced sweeping. As she walked away, I glared at her. Glancing about the room for the very first time, I noticed others who were also in pajamas, moving about to accomplish various chores.

Later I found myself sitting in a circle with 10 other patients as a nurse led us in discussion. My arms were folded. My mind was closed, a scowl set on my face. I was 38 years old. I had held a number of responsible positions in the armed forces, yet emotionally I had now regressed to the stature of a small child. A secular humanist, I worshipped humanity, and in so doing also worshipped myself. But now the tin god that I had been all along was finally exposed. By failing to live up to my own expectations, I had fallen into a quagmire of pure misery and come perilously close to death.

The following day the psychiatrist insisted he would not return my meds. Instead he introduced me to a relaxation technique, which I fought against with all my might. The splitting headaches continued to hammer me, and I felt cheated and betrayed. As the second afternoon wore on, however, for the first time I indulged myself in the security of the ward. I began seeing myself as larvae inside a cocoon. The stress of the outside world seemed to slip away more and more.

However, when my wife and children arrived to visit, I felt very ashamed, like an animal on display in a cage. It was odd seeing them there; they seemed so out of place. And they appeared uncomfortable. My wife acted concerned and yet somehow betrayed. My children, lost and hurt, needed, I well knew, a steady hand at the wheel, a stronger person than I to help steer their lives. Instead, they were stuck with this sick man on a psychiatric ward who was even more lost than they. When they left, I still felt ashamed, but at the same time strangely relieved. No longer on display, I felt able to relax again. It was as if the stress of my responsibilities departed with them. Slowly, my depression began to slip away.

One of the patients in the ward was a young, pretty woman, aged 21 or so, who wore a constant frown, refusing to cooperate with the group. One night an alarm was sounded and the lights switched suddenly on. We sat up abruptly in our bunks, gazing groggily about. Moments later we heard the staff lead the young woman kicking and screaming down the hall. Word traveled that she was found attempting to hang herself. A chill passed through me. I wondered: *Will life end for me soon?* It had been several hours since the death wish last washed over me and I shuddered at the thought it may return. I didn't fall back asleep that night but instead sat and stared at the wall, cradling my head from the incessant pain.

Next morning we waited in a huddle at the back door in our sweatpants and sneakers. Soon we were marched across an open lot to a gymnasium. "Throw it back," shouted a nurse, tossing a volleyball my way. The ball bounced off my chest, but I refused to pick it up. Instead I squatted down on the floor, my back against the wall. Dropping my hands into my lap, I stared fixedly at them. If I focused hard enough, I knew this world around me would slowly fade away; then it would be only me again, one solitary figure against the wide universe, the way it was meant to be.

At that moment, I found the prospect of playing any kind of game completely repulsive. I wanted to shrink away into my own misery, to sulk and soak myself in the familiar soup of self-pity. The toes of another pair of shoes touched mine, yet still I did not look up. I imagined no one was there; if I imagined hard enough, I speculated, perhaps it would be so.

"Get up!" the nurse ordered. "Get up!" he said again when I didn't respond. "Get up! Now!" he snapped. This time my reflexes demanded that I look up. I did, but immediately turned my face away.

It was my father again standing over me, berating me when I was a small child. It was the master sergeant at Bien Hoa Air Base demanding more from me than I was able to give as mortar rounds slapped the life out of young men all about me. It was my current ship's captain wanting me to produce even now although I had somehow lost my way.

I unknowingly craved a relationship with my Creator, and the resulting emptiness welling up within me was swallowing me whole. With no God, I was without a reliable frame of reference; rather I was like a pendulum caught up in a storm, swinging erratically, or a gyroscope with no inertial coordinates. I did not know who I was. I was an exhausted, thirsty man lost in a desert with no compass and no will.

I glared up at the nurse. Since I behaved like a four-year-old, he treated me as such. "Either you get up now or I will pick you up!" he snapped. The breadth of his shoulders and the stern gaze of his eyes told me he was serious. I noticed that all the others were on the court. Slowly, but with an audible sigh of annoyance, I pulled myself erect and dragged myself toward them.

I generally enjoyed volleyball. In fact, ordinarily it was my favorite sport to play; consequently, I soon found myself watching the game. Someone tossed the ball toward me and it glanced off my shoulders. The players gazed at me accusingly, and their expectant looks finally melted my will. Soon I was bounding across the court with them. As I did so, my depression mysteriously lifted.

That night I listened as screams emanating from the adjoining room mingled with the shouts of the nurses. Attentive to the noise, I lay in the dark, thumbing a novel by Kurt Vonnegut and pondering the purpose of living. Search as I would, I could find none. Like a character from Vonnegut's *Mother Night*, I thought I may slip off into some surreal netherworld, never to return.

For to live is but to know pain—just listen to the screaming down the hall! Let us slip away into a peaceful demise, a state of nonexistence, which brings surcease from the pain of living! Let us go! Shuddering in the dark, I drifted off to sleep. The book fell to the floor with a sound as soft as wind rushing through the willows.

Over the following days, I opened up more and more, chatting with the other patients. I even found myself whistling while doing the daily chores. I became more amiable during the family visits, and my wife commented on how relaxed I had become. But I knew the change was due to enforced separation from my family. Absent from them, I was free from my stress. I felt so guilty around them, knowing I wasn't measuring up to the standards I had set for myself, the standards I knew they deserved. I was an inept father and husband, but I knew of no way to improve. It was the helplessness I felt in the face of that challenge that prompted me to withdraw and tempted me to end my life.

As I pondered this, I found myself slipping again into my dismal hideaway, the state of pure despair. Sharing in the group one evening, I talked about my recurring vision of the two cities in the sky, mounted far, far above my head, yet within my line of sight. As my perception telescoped out and in, I saw the cities' inhabitants close up, then at a distance.

The residents of one city suffered immensely. In the other city, just across the divide, people partied away in complete abandon, apparently oblivious of the plight of the others; out of sight, out of mind! I witnessed both populations, yet remained powerless to make a difference. I wrung my hands. My empathy with the sufferers, along with my sense of helplessness in the face of it all, was driving me mad! I was driven to despair over my inability to effect a balance, to take from those with much in order to share with those who had little, so that some who were dying might live, so that some who were suffering unbearably might suffer less.

"Can't you see?" I screamed to the wealthy people. "Can't you see the plight of those suffering millions? Don't you care one little bit at all?" Despite my protests, however, they remained unmoved. In fact, it was as if they did not hear me at all, as if they were in a soundproof bubble, oblivious not only of the plight of the needy but of my concerns as well. It was the double curse of both my awareness of the distress and my seeming helplessness in the face of it all that was driving me insane.

As I stopped speaking and my vision of the ethereal cities faded slowly away, I became aware of the strained and troubled faces of the people in my group. My gaze settled finally on the annoyed expression of the nurse. She frowned, and her eyes flashed as she snapped: "If you *continue* to go on like that, thinking and talking like that, you *will* go insane!" Startled at the curtness of her comment, I took a hard look at her and knew she meant what she said. It was as if I were suddenly doused in the face with ice-cold water. The full implications of her statement hit me hard, reverberating for a long time through my mind.

After the session concluded, I kept pondering her words: "If you *continue* to go on like that, thinking and talking like that, you *will* go insane." I received several clear and definite messages from this statement. One was reassuring: I was *not yet* insane! The other was a warning: if I continued to think and talk the way I was doing, then I *would* go insane. I also read into it a third message: if I did go insane, there may be *no coming back*. Mulling her statement over, I found a fourth implication: *I was worth saving!* The nurse cared! She cared about me, at least enough to warn me! She did this—even though I believed I was worthless, worth not much more than a worm!

I knew I had to make up my mind quickly about what I was going to do next, before it was too late! A chill passed over me. The nurse's stark, sincere assessment gripped my attention like nothing else had. I believed her, and the full implication terrified me. But there was still a chance, I repeated to myself—a chance for life! I steadfastly made up my mind to head for that goal post. It was as if I had been searching for a thread, any thread to which I could cling—and had found it!

A few days later, I was released. Over the days that followed, I worked hard at solidifying my grip on life, but ultimately failed. It's impossible to find a solid purpose for living when there is no sense of true north in one's world, no trustworthy frame of reference. Search as I might, I was unable to come up with a clear purpose for my existence. Consequently, as the weeks and months went by, I found myself once again headed down that slippery slope toward the slough of despond, leading ultimately to the desert of despair!

Not long afterward, my wife and I divorced. I moved into a noncommissioned officer (NCO) barracks on base with just a few meager possessions: my books by Freud (I read and reread *The Future of an Illusion,* which purports all religion to be just that: an illusion); Erich Fromm's *Man for Himself* (this book presenting Fromm's humanistic philosophy served as my bible); and Ernest Becker's *The Denial of Death* (my second bible, if I had one). These I kept by my bedside at all times.

BIBLE SELECTION

"For this people's heart has become calloused; they hardly hear with their ears, and they have closed their eyes. Otherwise they might see with their eyes, hear with their ears, understand with their hearts and turn, and I would heal them" (Acts 28:27 NIV).

REFLECTION

During this time, I was weighed down by the awareness that many crucial responsibilities involving my loved ones rested upon me and me alone; yet without Christ in my life, the only resources on which I could lean were my own strength and that of others like myself—all so finite.

Being unsaved is to always be in fear of the flames of hell waiting around the next corner. This is true even if the unsaved person professes no faith in either a heaven or a hell. As an atheist I inflicted great pain on those who meant the most to me, but I couldn't stop myself. And the backlash of that pain was horrendous. I was so enwrapped in self-pity (which has been called egoism turned inside out), that it took all my attention. I was angry at myself and I took it out on those nearest me, hurting them even more. But the awareness of what I was doing produced more guilt than I could handle. And all the time I was feeling the flames of hellfire flickering at the soles of my feet, producing excruciating pain—hence the source of my dilemma!

Dear Jesus, when you came into my life you gave it meaning. I finally had a reason to live, something I so direly needed! It was the disparity between what I knew intuitively—that I am made for more than this world—and the mindset which ruled me—that I am but a random product of mindless nature—that was driving me insane! It was not until in despair I turned my life and will over to you, the true God, that the tortuous despondency vanished. Dear Lord, I can never thank you enough!

In the precious name of Jesus Christ my Savior I pray. Amen.

CHAPTER SEVENTEEN

To Live or To Die?

IN THE SUMMER OF 1986, I bared my heart (a rare occasion!) in a telephone conversation with my brother Dale, a Freewill Baptist minister. After I told him of my anxiety and my pervasive feelings of discontent, he said something that, surprisingly, stuck with me: "There is real peace to be found in Jesus Christ." At the time I flung off the remark, chuckling; I let him know in no uncertain terms that his comment was lost on me! I was too smart, you see, to swallow such nonsense, such fantasy. However, I was to turn to those very words soon afterward.

A year after my discharge from the psychiatric ward, parked late one night on a remote side street, I suddenly felt again those old familiar feelings of despair descend upon me. Like long lost friends they clung to me, though I shivered from the sensation. I remember the night as vividly as if it were yesterday. I was reviewing the state of my life: the repeated clashes with my ex-wife, the seeming meaninglessness of my work in the Navy. I saw myself as a total failure and was filled with a convincing sense of the purposelessness of living.

Though I tried desperately to fling it off, the extent of my self-hatred rose to a crescendo. My despair seemed an external power over which I had no control, and it came in such full force that I felt I could no longer fend it off! Panicking, I gripped the steering wheel so tightly that I felt my fingers might sink into it. Then a sharp stab of fear pierced my heart as I hunkered down for the deathblow!

Though my eyes were dry and I made no sound, I sat hunched over that night in the cab of my car and inwardly wept. In my mind I was brought back to a time when I was 15 years old, the last time I allowed sobs to rack my body as a maelstrom pummels a ship at sea. Turned and tossed by internal forces over which I had no control, I finally surrendered that hot summer day and sobbed with all my might before my parents. Though I cannot remember the circumstances—why it was that I lost control and began sobbing so intensely—I do recall my father's reaction, the words which struck me like boulders: "There you go again. You're 15 years old, blubbering like a baby. When are you going to grow up and behave like a man? Get out of my sight until you quit your blubbering!"

My face buried in my hands, I cried uncontrollably, my tears flowing through trembling fingers—for I was sincerely, though vainly, attempting to stop. I shuffled from the room and out the screen door. In a fury at my inability to quit weeping, I flung myself against the back wall of the house, sliding down to a squatting posture on the grass as the crying shook my body with pure brute force.

My father's hammering words achieved their purpose. I subsequently internalized a life-motto: to stand strong as a man in the world, I must never weep, for to weep shows weakness. A real man never cries. To do so is shameful, therefore one must always control oneself. An atheist, I had learned to apply this principle quite literally: I had to control myself—I and no other! It was I and I alone against the whole wide world! From somewhere deep within myself, I had to muster forth the strength to carry on. In the face of the greatest challenge, I, all by myself, had to stand strong.

What is it that will prompt a person to consider the unthinkable? To open up their mind to a wholly new paradigm? To step outside a comfort zone so entrenched that to go contrary to it is like fighting quicksand? In other words, what is it that will prompt one to change 180 degrees, to totally reverse oneself?

One such force is the fear of death. And this was my motivation that night when, parked in my car, for the first time I reconsidered that fateful decision made a quarter century earlier—that there is no God in the world. As the irresistible drive toward self-destruction engulfed me, consuming my very will, my brother's reassuring words mysteriously floated back to me: "There is true peace to be found in Jesus Christ." And I cried out to the Lord, just as Peter did as he sank into the sea: *"Lord, save me!"* (Matt. 14:30). For you see, when I thought that I had finally exhausted all my resources—that there were absolutely none at all remaining—the arrogance which had defined my personality for so long completely evaporated. Though it took 25 long years, I learned then that, amazingly, God had never given up on me; the Lord rescued me *"like a burning stick snatched from the fire"* (Amos 4:11 NIV), and I will be forever grateful!

I consciously acknowledged: *The death wish is winning, and I don't want to die!* My brother's unsolicited words were now the single straw at which I grasped. *Just what if all the Bible-thumpers are correct? I asked myself. I've exhausted all other avenues. There's nowhere else to turn, no one remaining on whom to call except this God in whom so many seem to believe. It would be absurd to give up, to die, without giving this possibility at least one chance.*

Then, mysteriously, a Scripture verse surfaced from somewhere deep in my memory: *Be still and know that I am God* (Ps. 46:10 KJV). As I recalled the verse, like the obedient child I was when I first heard it, I clasped my fists together and prayed silently: *God, if there's the remotest chance you do exist, please let me know you now. Just show me you are real, for I do not want to die!* Shuddering, as the waves of despair washed over me the way ocean waves overtake a drowning man, I voiced silently, slowly and repeatedly the words: *I will be still and know that you are God.*

Then, when I thought I could fend off the suicidal impulses no longer, I was able—for a fraction of time—to still my mind. Suddenly, shockingly, I became vividly aware of God's precious presence with me—a warm, reassuring, ever so compassionate and welcome presence! How can I explain what it feels like as an adult to personally encounter God for the first time? How can anyone describe such a dramatic and overwhelming personal experience? Let me begin by acknowledging it was a warm, warm feeling of familiarity—for I had known his presence as a small child, though I had completely forgotten him. On the other hand, this experience was also very different: I had since known life's hard knocks—a devastating war experience and a heart-rending divorce—therefore I saw God through very different eyes. I saw him as the loving presence he had always been, but also as a fountain of grace freeing me from a crushing burden of guilt, a prison of my own making; a counsel to guide me through muddied waters; a protector from a threatening world; and a source of inner peace in the path of the storm.

When I realized that night that God himself shared the cab with me, when his Spirit felt as palpable to me as the sensations of sight and sound and touch are to my physical body, a bolt of sheer energizing power shot through me! And I was overcome by waves of refreshing grace. Like Jacob at Bethel I realized: *"Surely the Lord is in this place, and I wasn't even aware of it!"* (Gen. 28:16 NLT). Floating down a river of forgiveness, I could not believe my good fortune.

The awareness of God's indisputably strong and powerful presence was so very welcome! There he was, invisible to the naked eye but very visible to the eyes of faith. I opened the door of my mind but a fraction and he stepped in. I was awed at his presence! *Oh, Lord!* my soul exclaimed. *Thank you for your patience. Forgive me for my horrendous errors. Please give me another chance. And I will do the very best I can to serve you all the rest of my days!* And I meant it with all of my heart.

Aloud I exclaimed again and again: "God does exist! God does exist! I was wrong all along! Praise God, I am no longer all by myself in a losing battle against the evil and ugliness of the world; it is now God and I together! I don't have to die! I can live!"

BIBLE SELECTIONS

"Are you tired? Worn out? Burned out on religion? Come to me. Get away with me and you'll recover your life. I'll show you how to take a real rest. Walk with me and work with me—watch how I do it. Learn the unforced rhythms of grace. I won't lay anything heavy or ill-fitting on you. Keep company with me and you'll learn to live freely and lightly" (Matt. 11:28-30 MSG).

What a wretched man I am! Who will rescue me from this body of death? Thanks be to God—through Jesus Christ our Lord! (Rom. 7:24-25 NIV).

REFLECTION

As I think back to my state of mind during the days and weeks leading up to my conversion experience and compare that to what I felt afterwards, I am awed and amazed at the contrast. No wonder I fell so in love with God: I was such a wretched man! And he saved me—saved me from myself—for today I know it was I myself turning the vise grip that was crushing the very life out of me; I just didn't know how to stop!

I've often wondered why God accepted my plea at age 39, considering all that I had said and done, after the way I had scorned him for so long. But, praise God, he did accept my plea! He accepted me unconditionally the way a loving, caring parent accepts a crying, kicking baby in its crib, an infant who knows no better.

But I was no infant! I did know better! I cannot say, like Paul, *I was shown mercy because I acted in ignorance and unbelief* (1 Tim. 1:13 NIV), for I was not ignorant. Praise the Lord for his wonderful mercy! *Give thanks to the Lord for he is good. His love endures forever* (Ps. 136:1 NIV).

For the one thing I knew immediately, beyond any shadow of a doubt as the Lord cradled me that night: I knew he cared for me. He wasn't about to punish me as I had feared for my wrong behavior, which had left so many casualties in its wake. As I felt the warmth of God's unsurpassable love embracing me, I marveled at the wonder of this deep love. God's unassuming acceptance of me awed me more than I can say. I was immensely grateful.

Men and women out there, perhaps you haven't come as despairingly as I to the very brink of suicide, but I know that many of you are very unhappy. I speak from rich personal experience as I advise you to fully trust yourself to God. He will not let you down. There is no longer any need to bask in your own misery, seeking consolation in something impotent and deceiving, whether it be food or alcohol or your own fleeting strength. And certainly you can't find it in another human being. The really wonderful thing is that, as you learn to love and trust God more and more, you learn to love and appreciate other people more also. This is what it really means to love them in the Lord.

Dear Lord, I know there are many in the world today who are going through misery similar to what I experienced. I pray that they, too, may come to accept and know your unconditional love—not question or doubt it, but just accept it and allow it to permeate their whole being. May they, too, know your wonderful and full salvation!

No longer the small child in the cove am I, yet you are the same Lord I knew then. Though I am taller today and have seen far more of the world, seen hunger and sorrow and evil of great extremes, you accepted this hurting soul, took him up into your bosom and enwrapped him in your love. Thank you, dear God, for your great and patient love—so very much more than I will ever deserve!

In the precious name of Jesus Christ my Savior I pray. Amen.

CHAPTER EIGHTEEN

A Second Chance

THAT NIGHT I TRADED A death wish for a decision for Christ. With him in my life, the despair began slipping away, and my desire to live was reclaimed. I had a new lease on life! A second chance! And I was ever so grateful.

Ecstatically, I turned the key in the ignition and headed down Interstate 805. Pulling off the highway 15 minutes later, I entered a shopping center where I knew a Dalton Bookstore remained open. Rushing to the Bible section, I explored it excitedly. When I had closed my mind to God as a child, I had only a vague impression of the Bible. I remembered the accounts of miracles—of Jonah and the whale, of Joshua ordering the sun to stand still, of the Genesis account of creation; in short, I knew just enough to mistakenly equate the biblical accounts to mythology. They just couldn't be true, I had concluded.

But I had never discovered the harmony of Scripture, how Scripture traces the wonder of God's love and grace through the lives of his people, or the insightful teachings of Paul (who describes so credibly the fragmentation of our lives without Christ and how crucial a relationship with Christ is to becoming whole and sane). I knew nothing of the Adamic tendency within us all to sit in judgment upon God himself. I had no idea that my grueling experience of the past quarter century—the misery and despair of a life without God—is described so lucidly in the very book I had grown to disdain, the Holy Bible.

Running my fingers along the bindings of the books, I paused upon coming to a J.B. Phillips translation of the New Testament, *The New Testament in Modern English*. My curiosity was whetted; until then I had known only the King James Version. Thumbing through this New Testament, I became more and more excited. It was so much easier to get my tongue around the contemporary English language of this translation than the archaic words I had heard as a child.

That night, sitting up in bed, I read for the first time the words of 1 John 1:1-4 and I trembled at the thrill of the grand adventure upon which I was embarking:

> We are writing to you about something which has always existed
> yet which we ourselves actually heard and saw with our own eyes:
> something which we had opportunity to observe closely and even
> to hold in our hands, something of the Word of life! For it was
> life which appeared before us: we saw it, we are eye-witnesses
> of it, and are now writing to you about it. It was the very life of
> all ages, the life that has always existed with the Father, which
> actually became visible in person to us. We repeat, we really saw
> and heard what we are now writing to you about. We want you to
> be with us in this—in this fellowship with the Father, and Jesus
> Christ his Son. We write and tell you about it, so that our joy may
> be complete (Phillips).

The words jumped off the page at me! Reading them for the first time in my life, I found them crisp and new. It struck me that this was an eyewitness account handed down across the millennia:

> [W]e ourselves actually *heard and saw with our own eyes*:
> something which we had opportunity to *observe closely* and
> even to *hold in our hands.... we saw it, we are eye-witnesses of
> it....* It was the very life of all ages ... which actually *became
> visible* in person to us. We repeat, *we really saw and heard....*

As I reread the words, my heart skipped a beat. I understood that John was saying he had actually shaken the hands of the man Jesus Christ, felt the Lord's warm blood coursing through his veins. He had heard the audible voice of God as Jesus dialogued with him one on one and taught from the hillsides. He had seen the contours of the Lord's face—the arch of the nose, the line of the lips, the sparkle in the eyes. John was an authentic eyewitness to me and to so many others across the millennia. And because he recorded this account of his own personal experience with Jesus Christ, we too can share in a personal relationship with our Lord.

As I write these words, I am 57 years old; 18 years have elapsed since I first read this eyewitness account of John the apostle. Yet the electricity I felt that moment almost two decades ago still makes me quiver with excitement. I could not deny the ring of truth in the words. I had just finished reading Mark's gospel and flipped at random to these opening lines of 1 John. I was excited, ecstatic at the realization that God is in the world—I had been wrong all along! I cannot emphasize enough how important such a finding is to a person like me who had for years been fighting a losing battle all alone against a formidable world. Such a realization is like food to a starving man or a drink of cold water to one parched and dry in the desert! *As the deer pants for streams of water, so my soul pants for you, O God. My soul thirsts for God, for the living God* (Ps. 42:1-2 NIV).

The following evening, I picked up John's gospel. On coming to the account of the woman caught in adultery, I read with excitement these reassuring words of Jesus: *"Neither do I condemn you. Go home and do not sin again"* (John 8:11 Phillips). Reading this passage, tears mounted in my eyes; I got a glimpse of the grace of God. Mind you, I was a hard, calloused man; nothing could make me cry. But there in the privacy of my own room, I allowed myself at least a single tear. Burdened by over two decades of life without God, the accumulated sins of my lawless lifestyle so weighed me down that I struggled beneath an impossible burden. Physical and spiritual trauma are not that distinct from one another in terms of their impact. I was a severely tortured man.

Pondering the grace of God, I contemplated praying. I had only spoken the simple prayer in my car the night before. Now reading of God's grace and forgiveness, I wanted to properly say to him, "Thank you."

I glanced down at the floor where I felt I should kneel. Reflecting today, I recall the tremendous effort of will that first gesture took. I had not knelt in prayer for decades, therefore it all seemed faintly ludicrous to me. But, finally, I flung myself out of bed and knelt down awkwardly on my knees, my elbows resting on the mattress of my cot. Quietly I pondered, *What do I do next?* I hadn't a clue.

The hard truth then hit me squarely between the eyes. My dramatic encounter with God in the car was unique—a foxhole conversion experience. My first prayer was a spontaneous outcry, an eruption from deep down in my gut, a pure plea for help. I was making a choice between death and life; I picked life. God saved me from myself, from my deadly suicidal compulsions. Now that I had encountered God, I was bent on maintaining an effective relationship with him; I knew absolutely that my very life depended upon it.

Intuitively, I sensed that a daily dialogue with him was essential. This I was anxious to do, but I hadn't a clue how to proceed.

I wonder how unusual it is for a man or woman to experience a Christian conversion all alone—when it is just that solitary person and the Lord. One drawback to such a circumstance is that, as questions arise about prayer and other spiritual matters, there is no one to turn to—except the Lord himself. I knelt there for the longest time, and nothing seemed to happen. For 10 minutes, 15 minutes, 30 minutes I restlessly knelt, intermittently reading various verses from John. Finally I resigned myself to the fact that I was not going to succeed this night.

Over the days that followed, I continued to read and attempt to pray, still without success. For the first time that Sunday I visited the base chapel. It was a sparsely attended worship service, and I left feeling dry and dissatisfied. I met with the base chaplain, a young man, and shared with him my recent religious experiences. As I talked, he showed great surprise and was unsure of how to help me. Finally, I told him bluntly that there were three things I wanted: to learn how to pray, to get to know God better, and to find a church. At first he seemed at a loss, but he finally did something for which I will forever be grateful: he pulled from his bookcase a copy of F. Scott Peck's volume *The Road Less Traveled* and showed it to me, saying, "I'm afraid I can't let go of this copy; it is the only one I have. But I recommend that you read it. It's a bestseller and is available at any bookstore. I think you'll find in it the answers to many of your questions."

And he was right. As I read Peck's analysis, I became more and more convinced that there is a spiritual plane to the world, something I had denied all my adult life. And I unquestioningly accepted the biblical teaching of the synonymy of God and love. I grasped this link intuitively to be the universal tenet that explained everything; all else simply fell into place as this truth hit home for me. "I love you, too, Lord. I love you, too," I murmured again and again, searching for a way to continue my dialogue with him.

One Saturday, after spending the morning reading Peck's book and the Bible side by side—reading first one, then the other, alternately—I left the barracks, walking briskly toward the NCO club to have lunch. Richly sensing the fall breeze on my face and basking in the exciting revelations that my study was yielding, I felt suddenly as if I were high-stepping a full nine feet into the air. For so long I had been dragging myself about, half-buried beneath a mountain of guilt and shame; the discovery of how I might harness the very power of God himself in my existential battle against despair was a newfound freedom that I found exhilarating and almost intoxicating. As I sped into a jog, I felt as if I were straddling mountains beneath my feet.

It was two weeks after my dramatic first encounter with the Lord, two weeks of study and contemplation, before I dared broach the subject in a telephone conversation with my mother. I had waited to tell my parents for fear that what I was experiencing was ephemeral, a mere moment of emotional excitement that would pass. I had let my parents down so many times, I didn't want to take a chance on hurting them again. However, my assurance had only grown, and I knew beyond a shadow of any doubt that I had hit upon the truth.

From a pay phone at the NCO club I called her. "Mama, I have something to tell you: I have accepted Christ."

"What did you say?"

"Two weeks ago I accepted Christ."

She gasped. "You did? You were saved? Hallelujah! Son, do you have any idea how many years our church has been praying for you to make that choice? God has finally answered our prayers! Praise God!" This was the first that I had heard of this. Images of these faithful country folk flashed through my mind. I was very humbled and grateful.

I recounted what had transpired: my brother's words of encouragement, his suggestion of the way—peace with Christ; my prayer in my car; my adventure reading the Bible. I paused. "Mama, I have a question?"

"Yes?"

"How do you pray? I've been trying for days, kneeling by my cot, and nothing seems to happen."

She laughed and said, "Why, you just talk to God the way you do to a friend. Just open up your mouth and talk with him like that, or you can do it silently, either way."

I was startled. "Okay," I said. "You've been helpful."

As I left the phone booth, my mother's words kept running through my mind: *You just talk to God the way you do to a friend.* This sounded very odd to me. *We are speaking about the Creator of the universe! I am the creature. He is the Creator. Does the Creator condescend to befriend his creation? A man would never befriend something he created. God creates life. Does he really befriend the very life that he creates?*

I tried to make sense of the concept. On first hearing it, it seemed to me not unlike a bizarre science fiction twist. Then suddenly I recalled some words of Christ I had read recently: *"Greater love has no one than this, that he lay down his life for his friends"* (John 15:13 NIV). Abruptly the point hit me like a bullet between the eyes: God took on human form; he tasted death for all mankind; he took the punishment due us upon himself. The Creator died for his own creatures! He did lay down his life for his friends—and he considers me his friend! The enormity of the revelation, the grandeur of the epiphany, froze me in my tracks: Christ died for me, yes, even me, because he considers me his friend!

I was greatly humbled by this insight because for decades I had been a *very bad* friend—in fact, anything *but* a friend—to Christ. Moments later, kneeling by my bed once more, the passage from John 15 before me, I reread the words. Pondering them for a few minutes, I suddenly felt God's presence in the room quite vividly, that familiar presence from the cab of my car, and I trembled at the realization. Giddy, I began my prayer, speaking extemporaneously with my new friend. *Dear God, here is my situation. I know you know it already, but I want to talk about it with you, my friend.* And I dialogued with him; I bared my soul from the very core of my being. As I talked, I felt the tension in my body and the burning burden in my heart melt slowly away. Pausing, I laughed out loud from the pure joy of the experience: God accepted my burden! This is what it means to turn it over to God, I realized. "Thank you, Lord!" I cried aloud.

As air gushes forth from of a balloon, the remaining pressure left me. Exiting the building, I dashed down the street, my face into the wind. I skipped and leaped, feeling as if I were walking on air. "Thank you, God!" I shouted. People on the street stared at me, but I cared little what they thought—I was alive with Christ! I had learned how to talk with my friend! My wonderful, divine friend!

In just two weeks, my whole world was flipped upside down. Once a lonely, depressed human being, despairing even of living, I now had a friend in Jesus—the great God of the universe, no less! What better protector could I possibly have from the encumbrances of living? What better acquaintance to whom to bare the very depths of my soul? Flushed with the grandeur of the revelation, I longed to share my wonderful news!

Over the days that followed, the despair that had long haunted me met head on with my newfound source of power. I have described my vision of the two cities in the sky—one a city of impoverished masses and the other of privileged gluttons. I have also shared my vivid memories from the war, how they buffeted my mind at times least expected, spiriting me back to 1968 and moments long frozen in space and time. Having gazed into the eyes of emaciated men and women who appeared far older than their years and of listless toddlers whose dull eyes portended imminent death, I had long carried a burden for the enormous needs of the world. Having held dying young men in my arms, buddies whose gushing blood stained my clothes and hands, I had long carried a burden for those who died fighting wars. Because of the impotence I felt in the face of such great atrocities, these images, these horrors had long been crushing me. *Now that God is with me,* I reasoned, *I can finally make a difference! I can be of some help to those in great need!*

As I opened my burdened heart to Jesus, I was overjoyed to find that he shares these same burdens. He cares! In fact, he loves far more than I. I had long loved in the abstract but disliked people in the particular; God loves with no exceptions. He grieves for the tragedies that beset his creation. I rejoiced as I read:

> *Jesus went through all the towns and villages, teaching in their synagogues, preaching the good news of the kingdom and healing every disease and sickness. When he saw the crowds, he had compassion on them, because they were harassed and helpless, like sheep without a shepherd. Then he said to his disciples, "The harvest is plentiful but the workers are few. Ask the Lord of the harvest, therefore, to send out workers into his harvest field"* (Matt. 9:35-38 NIV).

Lord, I share your compassion for all humanity, I prayed. *Please make me one of the workers in your harvest field, not only to bring the good news of your love for all but also to help heal their manifold afflictions. There are so many who are harassed and helpless. Lord, please teach me to be a shepherd who will lead them to the Great Shepherd.* With this prayer, said on my knees in the privacy of my barracks room, I realized my calling to full-time ministry and embarked upon a search for a church.

BIBLE SELECTION _____

The cords of death entangled me;
the torrents of destruction overwhelmed me.
The cords of the grave coiled around me;
the snares of death confronted me.
In my distress I called to the Lord;
I cried to my God for help.

He reached down from on high and took hold of me;
he drew me out of deep waters.
He rescued me from my powerful enemy,
from my foes, who were too strong for me.
They confronted me in the day of my disaster,
but the Lord was my support.
He brought me out into a spacious place;
he rescued me because he delighted in me.

The Lord lives! Praise be to my Rock!
Exalted be God my Savior! (Ps. 18:4-6, 16-19, 46 NIV).

REFLECTION _____

When we attempt to compare a spiritual experience with an unspiritual one, to compare a real, personal, undeniable awareness of God's presence with an awareness, say, of a warm humid wind blowing in our face, it is very difficult to do so.

But I can share that a spiritual experience is more full, and far more convincing, than an unspiritual one. The five physical senses can be fooled, as we know from watching a magician at his trade. But what I experienced that evening was an out-and-out full awareness of God's presence with me. Have you had such an experience of God as well? A feeling of God's warm and gracious self fully embracing you, loving you, forgiving you, letting you know that everything is alright now because he is on the scene, he is right there with you and will remain with you? That was my experience, one that took me back across three decades to when I was a small child and he first held me in his arms:

We shall not cease from exploration
And the end of all our exploring
Will be to arrive where we started
And know the place for the first time.[14]

How great is the love the Father has lavished on us, that we should be called children of God! (1 John 3:1 NIV).

My response was one of jubilation, excitement, and deep and profound appreciation. I now knew there was someone in the world who loved me immensely despite all my shortcomings, all my grave errors, despite the hurt I had caused so many. And he was all-powerful, dependable, faithful, capable; therefore, I need be afraid no longer. I felt the embrace of his love in a wonderful, seemingly magical way.

Dear Lord, how wonderful was my discovery that you are a God of unconditional love. We tend to take it for granted, forgetting what it really means. My sins were so burdensome that their weight brought me to death's door. Yet you forgave them all!

Dear Lord, I am awed just to think you walked among us in human form once upon a time, that Peter and John and others felt the flesh of those arms and hands and observed the intelligent, deeply probing look in those eyes that saw everything! To think they spoke with you the way any person talks with another makes my spine tingle. Oh, how I would have liked to have been there!

But I am here with you now in the privacy of my living room late on a Sunday night, and I feel your presence as surely as I do the cup of tea that I am sipping and the feel of the computer keyboard beneath my fingers. I cannot deny your warm, embracing presence! You are as real to me in spiritual form as you were to John in physical form. Lord, I can't thank you enough for the gift of your presence with me.

In the precious name of Jesus Christ my Savior I pray. Amen.

PART III
THE SALVATION ARMY

CHAPTER NINETEEN

In Search of a Church

I FELT STRONGLY COMPELLED to share my newfound joy in Christ, for he had given me a new lease on life, a second chance at living! I turned in all sincerity to God and laid this question before him: *Lord, you have done so much for me! Thank you for saving my life! Now I deeply desire to do something for you in return. What can I do to express the extent of my appreciation to you?*

He replied: *Be content with your life, be considerate of others in everything you do, and continue to love me with all your heart.*

Of course I will, Lord, I responded. *I will always love and praise you; I cannot help but do so, for you have saved my life! But I want to do even more!* Then the words of an old hymn I had heard as a child popped into my mind: "He's got the whole world in his hands!" And I knew there was nothing I could give God that he didn't already have. Nothing except my right to myself! And this I had just given him. But I wanted to do still more! In my reading one day, I came upon these words of Christ in Matthew:

> "Come, you who have won my Father's blessing! Take your inheritance—the kingdom reserved for you since the foundation of the world! For I was hungry and you gave me food. I was thirsty and you gave me a drink. I was lonely and you made me welcome. I was naked and you clothed me. I was ill and you came and looked after me. I was in prison and you came to see me there…. I assure you that whatever you did for the humblest of my brothers you did for me" (Matt. 25:34-36, 40 Phillips).

The words leaped off the page at me! They hit home—an epiphany that set my heart dancing—and I understood that I should give my thanks offering to God by helping hurting people; this was my new purpose for living. I got down on my knees in the privacy of my barracks room and humbly thanked him for showing me the way.

There was no doubt in my mind that God was calling me to full-time ministry, and specifically to a pragmatic one. If someone had asked me at the time what I meant, I would have said something like this: "God is calling me to reach out to hurting and suffering people—to broken people! He is not calling me only to preach and pastor [which is what I thought a traditional minister primarily did]. Rather, I want to literally get sweaty and dirty helping others in great need!"

Within days I was making the rounds of the various churches in the San Diego area, seeking an opportunity for ministry, but with no success. The combination of worship and practical ministry appeared to be a rare commodity indeed.

But in early September 1986, while relaxing in the barracks lounge, flipping through a copy of *People Magazine*, a story caught my eye—an account of the recent election of Eva Burrows to the office of General of The Salvation Army. Dubbed the highest positioned female ecclesiastical leader in the world, her election to office made news. Reading with great interest, I discovered two things: (1) The Salvation Army is an integral part of the Christian church; (2) The Salvation Army is not your stereotypical church, but rather a movement strongly engaged in the practical ministry of helping hurting people in the name of Christ. My heart leaped! This was exactly what I was seeking!

Searching anxiously through a phone book, I found the number to the local Salvation Army facility, the San Diego Citadel Corps. The officer with whom I spoke invited me to the worship service the following Sunday. Over the next few days, I anxiously ransacked the city library, reading everything I could find about The Salvation Army. And the more I read, the more intrigued I became.

When I first set foot inside the San Diego Citadel Corps, I was a broken man. I was also a surrendered man, stepping out in faith into a brand new world. Like Kierkegaard's "knight of infinite resignation," I had given up the very thing I had hoped to keep, my right to myself, and consequently gained a connection with the divine.[15] *"He who loses his life for my sake will find it"* (Matt. 10:39 NKJV).

In seeking a church, I was looking for a safe place where I could regroup under the careful guidance of others who knew the way. A fire burned inside my heart, an open wound that would not heal. Recently bandaged with God's sweet love, this wound remained very tender and required much care.

Entering the chapel foyer, I was a wounded man needing nurture, a frightened man seeking succor.

I noticed first a tall, lame man greeting the others as they entered. When he spotted me, I glanced about nervously, unsure of whether to go or stay; he made a beeline for me with all the purposefulness of an angler flinging a fishing line into a lake. John Nute, recruiting sergeant, took his post quite seriously, moving briskly despite a leg stiff from a stroke which paralyzed one side of his body.

At our first encounter, I was taken aback by this afflicted man who had not a bone of shyness in his body. But his intentions quickly became clear. He wanted to ensure I felt welcome, got answers to all my questions, and would come back again. Within seconds he had recorded all my contact information and I had a copy of the corps schedule in hand. I found it as easy to talk with John as it was to breathe. Now that I had a responsive audience, words gushed from me like water from a geyser.

God used John to plant the bait, to let me know I was in the right place. What I saw when I looked at John was what he was—there was absolutely no pretense to the man. I knew instantly I could trust him.

The worship service was followed by an open air meeting, an outdoor worship service held in a courtyard area a couple of blocks from the corps. Following on foot behind the band members bearing their instruments in their arms, I felt like I was an actor in some foreign film, it was all was so very new to me. Meanwhile, John kept tabs on me, informing me where to stand and what to do, for I hadn't a clue. I quickly learned I need not be inhibited around him; John mentored me as easily and openly as if I were his brother, and like a sponge, I drank in all he taught.

Intrigued by the self-assurance the speaker displayed when sharing his testimony, I wondered when I would have such an opportunity, and whether I would have the nerve to speak when the opportunity came, for I still felt a certain squeamishness. Sharing this concern with John, he replied, with a twinkle in his eye, "Follow me. Do what I do."

As the speaker finished, I obligingly followed behind John as he moved amongst the crowd of onlookers, greeting strangers and handing out flyers. When the altar call was given and people moved forward to kneel at the drum, John was the first on the spot to pray with them. With butterflies in my stomach, I held back; yet John made it look so easy, as natural as combing one's hair. I spotted a man about my age, desperation evident in his manner, his grizzled face showing he hadn't shaved for days. I was gripped, however, by the look of utter despair in his eyes. I knew that look; I had been there ever so recently. Hesitantly, I knelt beside him and took his trembling hand. "Would you like me to pray with you?" I murmured.

"Please," he said.

The lines on the man's face, the grime on his clothes, the unkempt hair, but most of all, the humility evident in his demeanor, pricked my conscience like a needle. I knew we were two of a kind coming before the Lord.

"My name's Glen. What's yours?" I asked.

"Kevin," he said, with a break in his voice.

I prayed, "Lord, I come before you to ask your help in meeting Kevin's needs. Touch his heart, dear Jesus, and confirm in his heart that you are present with him this afternoon. He loves you and comes before you humbly to ask your forgiveness for his sins and for clarity about your will for his life." I asked Kevin if he would like to pray, and he did so, haltingly but sincerely, from the heart. That afternoon we felt the Spirit of God move marvelously amongst us. I thanked God for his love and for working in the life of my new acquaintance, whom I now clung to in prayer.

Kevin prayed, "It's been a long time since I've talked to you, God. But I never stopped loving you. I've been through some rough times lately, and I need you. Please help me."

As we stood, I squeezed his hand firmly, then wrapped an arm around his shoulders. At that moment, I knew he and I were at the center of a cosmic drama in which Christ had the leading role. Simultaneously, God confirmed me in my calling. I knew beyond a shadow of any doubt that I belonged in ministry to men like Kevin.

Walking along with the band members back to the corps, I was a very humbled person, in utter awe that God was using me! Even me! God was using this broken human being!

BIBLE SELECTION _____

I waited patiently for the Lord;
he turned to me and heard my cry.
He lifted me out of the slimy pit,
out of the mud and mire;

he set my feet on a rock
and gave me a firm place to stand.
He put a new song in my mouth,
a hymn of praise to our God.
Many will see and fear
and put their trust in the Lord.

Then I said, "Here I am, I have come—
it is written about me in the scroll.
I desire to do your will, O my God;
your law is within my heart" (Ps. 40:1-3, 7-8 NIV).

REFLECTION

I will never forget this first time I prayed with a seeking soul. A Christian for only a few weeks, still very shaky about things spiritual, my mind still untrained and untried, I held this beaten man's hand in mine and put my arm around him; I recognized him as a brother. Though I was nervous, one thing I knew for certain: the invisible God was there.

I had also recently been hurt to the core. My feelings were still raw, as if they had been seared with a red-hot iron. But it was sensitivity to such pain that gave me empathy with the broken man with whom I knelt. At a glance, I knew Kevin as a kindred spirit. God loved him dearly—of this I was deeply aware. God's love for me had been proven, and I knew I was no more special to God than Kevin. And because God loved him, so did I, for no servant is above his master (Matt. 10:24).

Dear Lord, thank you for the honor of bringing another before you in prayer. Kneeling at that open air meeting on the grass before the drum, I learned that your Holy Spirit is all-sufficient. Kevin was the first in a long succession of people with whom I have prayed since you saved me 20 years ago. And I thank you dearly for each new opportunity.

In the precious name of Jesus Christ my Savior I pray. Amen.

CHAPTER TWENTY

Gaining a Mentor

A FEW WEEKS AFTER I began attending the corps it was announced one morning in the worship service that John Nute, whose responsibilities included a Friday night donation solicitation route, needed a replacement driver. My hand shot up; the prospect of volunteering alongside John excited me. So began my adventure as his driver and escort on his weekly rounds of San Diego's card rooms and bars.

I watched intrigued the following Friday as he entered a bar to a rousing cheer, then emerged 20 minutes later, moneybag full, boisterous farewells following him out the door. My curiosity was whetted. At the next stop I asked if I might accompany him. Looking me up and down, John remarked, "Well, too bad you haven't finished your Salvation Army soldier classes, so you don't have a uniform yet. But come on in. I'll introduce you." Following as unobtrusively as possible, I watched enthralled as John passed from barstool to barstool, then made the rounds of the tables, shaking his tambourine, asking: "Help The Salvation Army?"

This had been John's route for a decade; he was a fixture on the circuit. Ten- and 20-dollar bills made their way in rapid succession from wallets and purses into his tambourine. He introduced me as the sailor who was soon going on to The Salvation Army School for Officer Training, the seminary where Salvationists prepare to become Salvation Army officers and ministers. Unquestioningly, the patrons welcomed me. "Any friend of John's is a friend of ours," they replied.

A woman's hand shot out, gripping John by the arm. He turned to see a longtime acquaintance with tearing eyes. "Alice!" he exclaimed. "What's wrong?" With a cry in her voice, the woman announced she had been diagnosed with cancer and solicited his prayers. Extracting a worn New Testament from his shirt pocket, John read aloud; then, taking her hands in his, he prayed a deep and heartfelt prayer. Conversation and laughter rose around us, but where John sat praying with Alice, something beautiful was going on; the spiritual and temporal planes intersected there.

Similar incidences took place as we visited bar after bar and card room after card room over the Fridays that followed. Soon I, too, was visiting with the people, not just lingering near like "John's bodyguard," as someone had joked. The backslapping and jovial humor were repeated again and again, as were the prayer requests; the heartbroken were quick to open up to John. But there were some negative reactions as well. John told me that over the years he had been assaulted several times in the bars.

One night, during the course of our rounds, a man gestured me over to where he was hunkered down on a barstool. Looking me directly in the eyes, he commented, "You've got a lot of nerve coming into a bar to solicit money, considering the position The Salvation Army has on drinking."

Without blinking an eye I replied, "Sir, among the many social service institutions which The Salvation Army runs are several alcohol and drug rehab centers. In fact, there is a large one here in San Diego. Who knows, you might be in need of their services one day. In that event, you might consider your contribution this evening as an investment in your future." I was startled at my words even as I said them; I wondered if I had gone too far.

The man appeared taken aback at first, but then his face brightened, and he chuckled. "A good reply," he said. "You know, you may just be right." With that, he extracted a 50-dollar bill from his wallet and handed it to me. I promptly deposited it in John's tambourine.

John mingled with the street people, his unpresuming manner opening doors wherever he went. I watched and marveled, filing away for future reference every lesson learned. Reeking from alcohol, an elderly woman with matted hair received him with a full embrace. As he devoured a watermelon salvaged from a dumpster, a raggedy man waved John over to sit with him. A prayer concern was voiced; John's hand gripped the man's shoulder, and he lifted his voice in prayer.

I loved those chilly San Diego nights as I shared with John my faltering Christian walk, the baby steps I was taking. Here was this broken human being with a deeply compassionate soul, reaching out to tend my fragile spirit. I saw you in him, Lord—there is no doubt in my mind. Because of his nonjudgmental manner and his crystal clear, rock-solid faith, I knew that when I looked at John I was seeing you.

BIBLE SELECTION _____

This is real love. It is not that we loved God, but that he loved us and sent his Son as a sacrifice to take away our sins. Dear friends, since God loved us that much, we surely ought to love each other. No one has ever seen God. But if we love each other, God lives in us, and his love has been brought to full expression through us. And God has given us his Spirit as proof that we live in him and he in us.... God is love, and all who live in love live in God, and God lives in them. And as we live in God, our love grows more perfect (1 John 4:10-13; 16-17 NLT).

REFLECTION _____

Dear God, thank you so much for the gift of John's presence in my life. I was a raw and broken human being when I made his acquaintance, and his influence upon me was immense. I was very sensitive in those days to the slightest hint of condescension and would have run if I had sensed it in John, but there was none to be found. Like you, Lord, he looked down on no one; though we are your creatures—you are our Creator—you do not look down on us. When John looked at me he saw a broken man who had admitted his wrongs, had turned them over to the Lord, and was now, like him, a member of the kingdom. I have often wondered why John was so completely accepting of me, and I keep coming back to the same answer: Lord, it was your Spirit at work in him.

Dear God, John is with you now, along with his beloved wife Ann. After a lifetime in your service, they are resting with you today. At a delicate time, when I could have gone in any direction, you placed John in my life and he showed me your heart. Thank you, Lord, for this priceless gift.

In the precious name of Jesus Christ my Savior I pray. Amen.

CHAPTER TWENTY-ONE

Reaching Out to Hurting People

AFTER I WAS SAVED, I left my self-centered nature behind—more or less. In retrospect, I realize I was still very much into myself. However, at the age of 40, for the first time in my life I was consciously looking for ways to help others, seeking nothing in return.

Therefore, when I heard that another corps member, Margaret Foster, was seeking someone to accompany her on league of mercy visits to the VA hospital in San Diego, I volunteered. The Salvation Army's program for organized visits to homes or institutions was exactly what I needed at the time.

One particular experience stands out strikingly: my visits with a wheelchair-bound elderly woman whose body was so gnarled and twisted by arthritis that she elicited grimaces from the unprepared. I had visited with Kathy Weston for three Sundays when one day I asked, "Kathy, what can we do for you that would be most meaningful?"

She looked me boldly in the eye. "I would dearly love to see the Pacific Ocean one more time. I haven't been outside these walls in over two years." As she talked, her face lit up. "But with these twisted legs of mine, what can I do?"

The excitement in her voice was palpable, but the frustration was equally pronounced. I asked, "Would you like us to give you a ride to the shore?"

"Oh, I would dearly love it!" she exclaimed. "But how would I get into your car?"

I thought for a minute. "I believe I can lift you ... if you trust me to."

Kathy shook her head doubtfully—it was evident she had reservations—but ultimately her intense desire to get out of the hospital, even for just a little while, won out. When the date rolled around, Margaret and I found her sitting up in her wheelchair, dressed for the excursion in a beautiful flowery pink dress, her face all aglow. However, as I wheeled her out the door to my

Toyota Tercel, for the first time I had my own reservations; I realized just how very twisted her limbs were!

Kathy studied my face nervously as slowly, cautiously I lifted her from the wheelchair, then set her sideways on the front passenger seat, her legs dangling in the air. So far, so good. But my greatest challenge loomed: how to get those arthritis-ravaged legs inside the car without hurting her.

I had turned her only a few inches when Kathy let loose such a howl of pain that a bolt of regret pierced me to the bone. I hastily apologized, then tried once more. Again she screamed. What to do? I was beginning, for the first time, to have real doubts as to whether the plan would succeed. "I'm so sorry," I stammered. "Do you want to forget the whole thing?"

Her tears fell in torrents. Nevertheless, she looked me directly in the eye. "Do it," she said. "I'm sorry. It hurts so. But please try again." I did, and again she howled. Finally, on the fourth attempt, I succeeded. As I slipped into the driver's seat beside her, she smiled encouragingly, her face now aglow in glad expectation.

Half an hour later I pulled the car off the side of the highway at a lookout point presenting a wide view of the Pacific Ocean. Kathy was in her glory, a picture of pure joy as she took it all in. For hours we chatted, reminisced, ate hot dogs and drank sodas, and watched the ships move in and out of the harbor below. The whole sky was awash with seagulls.

Basking in this moment, Kathy seemed to be 20 years younger, her face illuminated as she reminisced about more pleasant times when she and her husband had reared two daughters. One of their favorite pastimes, she said, was to sit on their patio both morning and evening looking out to sea, watching the ships as we were doing now.

As we gazed out to where the sea met the sky, Margaret, Kathy, and I drank in a multihued, flamboyant sunset. The whole sky around us turned a lovely purple and orange. We watched the colors emerge, blend, and change before our eyes. "What a lovely show the Lord has provided for us!" Kathy commented thoughtfully. She turned to me with an expression that spoke volumes, and the full extent of her gratitude hit home; the contented, beaming look upon her face was worth a million dollars. The joy of helping others—such a new experience for me—was almost overwhelming. I had never dreamed such joy existed!

The delightful afternoon with Kathy invigorated me. It also bolstered me, I think, for my encounter with an atheist the following week. The rich experience with God at that point overlooking the Pacific buttressed my spirit and empowered me to field the pejoratives that spewed forth like venom from the mouth of the atheist.

I met him as he was being wheeled out to the terminal patient ward. Talking with the man, I found he had only months to live. Most of the patients on this ward, recognizing my Salvation Army uniform, knew I was a Christian and, by and large, welcomed the sharing of Scripture and prayer. But Jim was different. On my initial encounter, I was completely taken aback by his abrasive opposition to my newfound Christian faith.

"Don't give me any of that religious crap!" he snapped.

Startled at the vehemence in his voice, I agreed to avoid the topic if that was what he wished, and asked him simply how he was doing. "Not so hot," he replied in a gravelly voice, explaining he had been diagnosed with emphysema and was near the end of his "run," as he called it. "But, what the hell! Life's dealt me a lousy hand, anyhow. I'm ready to bow out," he said.

Using sentences rife with profanity, the veteran went on to explain that he was angry with his family, as well as with life in general. He refused to believe, he said, in any God who would permit the ugliness that pervades this world. He was outraged at all that defined his existence!

I told him my story, and he listened intently. "The difference between you and me," he replied when I finished, "is that you have bought into the lie! There is no God! You've accepted the illusion because it provides you with a sense of serenity and security—that's all!"

I talked with him at length, yet he persisted in his attitude. He was angry. He was bitter. There appeared to be nothing I could do to change his mind.

Week after week I visited Jim on the ward. One day he mentioned he actually looked forward to my visits. I told him I was glad, that I very much enjoyed my visits with him as well. Another day he opened up his mind enough to allow me to pray with him. Smiling weakly when I finished, he remarked, "I still don't believe in your so-called God, but thanks anyway for the prayer."

On my next visit, I found his bed empty. Jim passed the night before, I was told. A chill passed over me. And I prayed, *Dear God, thank you for bringing me to this man. I hope and pray that he found his peace. Thank you, Lord, for your love.*

BIBLE SELECTION _____

Lord, our Lord, how majestic is your name in all the earth!

You have set your glory above the heavens.
Through the praise of children and infants
you have established a stronghold against your enemies,
to silence the foe and the avenger.
When I consider your heavens, the work of your fingers,
the moon and the stars, which you have set in place,
what are mere mortals that you are mindful of them,
human beings that you care for them?

You have made them a little lower than the heavenly beings
and crowned them with glory and honor.
You have made them rulers over the works of your hands;
you put everything under their feet:
all flocks and herds, and the animals of the wild,
the birds of the sky, and the fish in the sea,
all that swim the paths of the seas.

Lord, our Lord, how majestic is your name in all the earth! (Ps. 8 TNIV).

REFLECTION _____

Sitting in my car that Sunday afternoon, drinking in the mesmerizing sunset with Margaret and Kathy, was one of the most uplifting experiences of my life, for the look of pure joy Kathy gave me was incomparable. I was struck by the fact that the little things many of us take for granted are priceless to those who don't have them. Lord, thank you for the lesson of that moment—that we each have it in our power to make such a difference in the life of another, and with so little effort! There is no excuse for us doing nothing—not when you have done so very much for us!

I saw myself in Jim. He is the man I might have become if I had not given my heart to the Lord when I did. I ached so to get inside his mind and show him the way to the truth by imparting to him the benefit of my own experience with God—something that cannot be done.

The bottom line is that we know who God is by virtue of our own experience with him, not someone else's. The atheist does not yet know what we know because he has not yet been where we are. This is the reason we use the language of faith, *the substance of things hoped for, the evidence of things not seen* (Heb. 11:1 KJV). Through faith we enter into an experience of God, who is the sole source of all we know via our five senses.

Therefore, the only "proof" of God I could offer Jim the atheist was the "evidence" of my own testimony of God's love and grandeur, which I gleaned through personal experience with him. For Jim's sake, I hope that was enough.

Thank you so, Lord, for the grace you have shown me in giving me the wondrous gift of *"more and better life than [I] ever dreamed of"* (John 10:10 MSG).

In the precious name of Jesus Christ my Savior I pray. Amen.

CHAPTER TWENTY-TWO

A Challenge in Self-Control

AS I WATCHED THE WOMAN emerge from beneath the bridge, holding a toddler by the hand and cradling an infant in her arm, my heart leaped. *So this is what it means to be a Salvationist,* I thought, *to offer sandwiches and a cup of soup in Christ's name.*

As we pulled the canteen to a stop at the edge of the park, our last stop of the night, the woman rushed to get into the line that was forming. Already there were at least 20 men and women jostling to get ahead of one another. "Easy, easy. There's plenty to go around," said Mark, the man working with me. He had done this many times.

"My name's Glen. What's yours?" I asked the rough-looking gentleman who was first in line.

"I'm Don," he replied. "You folks are a little early tonight."

"A bit," I said as I helped Mark break out the equipment. Soon I was helping serve. Hollow-eyed and gaunt, Don looked as if he needed several meals to get some meat on his limbs. He was around 40 and his clothes were dirty and torn. He had at least a four-day old beard and an eye twitch that wouldn't stop. I had heard that a lot of drug addicts camped out in the parks. Some of the homeless tonight carried blankets over their shoulders and some wore them as coats. The parks were their homes. Older alcoholics, haunted war-veterans among them, were in the line. Some men. Some women. The wild look in the eyes of many revealed that their minds were a million miles elsewhere; they were not in tune with reality.

We offered each person a sandwich, a bowl of soup, and a cup of coffee. Water, milk and juice were also available. The line continued to grow. I was beginning to wonder if we had enough for everyone when a grizzled, burly man stepped forward. I recognized him immediately; he was one of the first I had served this evening. "May I have a sandwich and coffee?" he demanded.

"Sir, I wish I could help you. But we're running out of rations. I served you earlier, and the people behind you have had nothing."

"So?" he stated emphatically. "I'm next in line and I'm asking you for a sandwich and coffee."

My patience was wearing thin. "Sir, I'm sorry. I can't help you."

His eyes flashed and his jaw clenched. Abruptly he stepped forward so that his face was just a foot or so from mine—then he spat on me!

Time stood still. Spittle streamed down my forehead and nose. I saw red; I felt violated. Deep resentment mounted within me, and I was suddenly seized with an intense desire to strike or curse the man. Wiping my handkerchief shakily across my face, I eyed him standing there, leering, clearly seeking to provoke me to anger. Silently I prayed: *God, help me to behave like Christ toward this man. Help me to control my temper.* A sensation of deepest warmth and the assurance of God's protective presence enveloped me. Through his grace I was able to respond: "God bless you, sir."

The leer instantly vanished, replaced by a scowl. With an oath, the man stomped off, leaving me staring blankly after him, handkerchief still in hand. *Thank you, Lord!* I prayed, for I knew I would never have reacted this way before I had come to know Christ. *And dear Jesus, please touch this man's heart. I pray that he will come to know you and one day find your peace.*

I turned my attention back to the line of people. It was twilight. Darkness would overcome us momentarily. As the woman with the two children approached, my heart went out to her. There was a frightened look in her eyes; her teeth were bad and her cheeks hollow. The face of the toddler clinging to her skirt was dirty, his clothes torn. I couldn't help but wonder what their story was. Handing her the food, I asked a few questions: What were her needs? Where was she from? She was friendly and willing to talk, though there was a tone of desperation in her voice. She was driving through on the way to a relative in the next state when her car broke down. It was an old clunker put together with haywire; there was no saving it, she said. For two days she and her little ones had been stranded. The last of her money was gone, and she didn't know what to do.

I told her to stand by, that I thought I could help her. As I served the remaining people the last of the food stock, darkness enveloped the park. In the moonlight, I found a pay phone and called the Salvation Army family shelter. They had room; send them right over, they said. When I shared the good news, the woman's face lit up. "Oh, thank you! Thank you!" she exclaimed. Calling a taxi at my own expense, I saw the little family off.

As I watched the taxi disappear into the dark, I glanced back out at the park where a few people were still eating. The van was closing up. I got in beside the driver and prayed, *Dear Jesus, thank you for a good day. Thank you for giving me the strength to react as I did when the stranger spat on me. Thank you for using me to help the mother and her children find shelter, and for feeding so many this evening. Thank you, Lord, for using someone like me, who has done so much wrong, to bring a little good into the world.*

BIBLE SELECTION

Trust in the Lord and do good;
dwell in the land and enjoy safe pasture.
Delight yourself in the Lord
and he will give you the desires of your heart.

Commit your way to the Lord;
trust in him and he will do this:
He will make your righteousness shine like the dawn,
the justice of your cause like the noonday sun.

Be still before the Lord and wait patiently for him;
do not fret when men succeed in their ways,
when they carry out their wicked schemes.
Refrain from anger and turn from wrath;
do not fret—it leads only to evil (Ps. 37:3-8 NIV).

REFLECTION

Though it was 20 years ago this month, I remember like it was yesterday the heated moment when the leering stranger spat on me, for there is something about the feel of another person's saliva dripping down your face that remains with you; there are few things people find so insulting. My immediate impulse was to reply in kind or, even worse, to respond with a blow—a slap or a swing of the right fist against the man's jaw.

But I didn't. Why didn't I? Or why did I not at least emit a tirade of unchristian-sounding speech that would have been heard from a block away?

The only answer is that I was no longer the man I had been just a few months prior.

I had been near death—both physically and spiritually—and I had fallen at the feet of Christ in exhaustion. Christ picked this broken human being up from off the ground and performed spiritual heart surgery of such magnitude that the angry man who had been there was transformed (2 Cor. 5:17). Consequently, when wiping the spittle from my face and seeing in the shadows of that sunset the wild, menacing leer in the man's eyes, the anger his act generated vanished as quickly as it had come. I prayed, *God, help me to behave like Christ toward this man,* and the Lord answered my prayer.

Dear Lord, thank you for changing me from an angry, bitter person to one who can respond to gross insults with the demeanor appropriate for a Christian. Today, when I meet men and women who remind me of the person I used to be, I am overcome with gratitude to you for setting me free from those chains, the chains of obsessive selfishness.

Lord, I've come so far; yet I still have far to go. May I remain a humble student in your classroom for the rest of my life.

In the precious name of Jesus Christ my Savior I pray. Amen.

CHAPTER TWENTY-THREE

The Soul of a Killer

THE MAN'S RED HAIR was striking, yet it was the stark contrast between that flaming head of hair and the hardened expression upon his face that first gripped me.

I was lounging on a Saturday night at a Salvation Army Adult Rehabilitation Center (ARC) men's residence. I had recently arrived from the School for Officer Training, where I had been ordained and commissioned as a lieutenant in The Salvation Army, and I was on fire for the Lord! Taking up residence in the facility's guest apartment, I was hoping the proximity would give me an opportunity to get to know the men.

The administrator had introduced me during the morning devotions, so when I slipped down to the game room, though I was no longer in uniform, all eyes turned towards me. Glancing up from their table games and conversations, the men followed me with their eyes until, like deer watching a potential predator until fully convinced it isn't a threat, they concluded I was harmless.

Aware of this, I tried to appear at ease among them—which wasn't difficult, since I truly did feel more comfortable among them than even among the Salvation Army officers I knew. Like many of these men, I too had been broken. In fact, I was still reeling from the experience. I had come face to face with my own powerlessness, and it was from that dark place that I had reached out to God. Now I too was working a recovery program; like many of them, I was learning to lean daily upon my Higher Power, Jesus Christ. They were my brothers, and if they did not yet know Jesus, I was prepared to introduce them to him.

Alone at the pool table, I was idly shooting a few balls when "Red" Andersen approached. Spying him behind me out of the corner of my eye, I instantly did a double take. Red's wavy, flaming hair contrasted sharply with the dispassionate expression in his eyes and the deep wrinkles on his face—

the product of a lifelong smoking habit—so that he looked unreal, almost as if he had stepped from the pages of a comic book.

I recognized the calculating look he gave me. He was sizing me up, attempting to get a read on me. I nodded, then smiled as I saw the suspicion in his eyes slowly recede. I felt certain that he had a tragic past, and I felt a warm kinship with the man. I guessed him to be about 60. "Want to play a game?" I asked.

"Sure," he grunted, picking up a stick. We passed the following hour shooting pool and joking with one another. Red had a hundred questions for me, all of which I answered matter-of-factly. Though I was curious about him, I asked him nothing, yet through his comments learned that he had just recently checked into the program. He shared how difficult it was for him to put up with the "immature behavior" of his dorm mates, who were for the most part methamphetamine addicts. "Those brats act like they're 12 years old," he quipped.

I reminded him that a person pretty much ceases growing emotionally the moment he or she begins abusing drugs. Once they check into the program, clean and sober perhaps for the first time in decades, addicts pick up emotionally where they left off when they began their habit. This, of course, makes it hard for the more mature people around them, like Red, who developed their chemical dependency later in life.

Red listened attentively and nodded; what I said was congruent with his experience. He smiled for the first time, apparently pleased with me. It was as if I had passed some kind of a test. Now he opened up like a geyser, sharing a great deal of personal information. I assumed a nonjudgmental posture, flattered that he trusted me this much after knowing me only a few minutes. He told me that, following a lengthy prison stint, he had checked directly into the program for fear he would revert to drinking.

Around 10 p.m., I remarked it was time for me to hit the hay, sharing with him how much I had enjoyed our conversation. As I turned to leave, I noticed a flicker in his eyes, an indication that he had something more he wanted to share. I glanced back. He was squinting in my direction, his brow creased, a contemplative expression on his face. He suddenly noticed me watching him and turned away self-consciously. Something was burdening him, I knew, something he wanted to get off his chest, but he wasn't sure that he wanted to make his move just yet. I respected his rights; the choice was his.

Twenty minutes later a knock sounded at my apartment door. I answered it in sock feet, wearing just a t-shirt and jeans. There stood Red, looking quite morose and troubled. When he spoke, I sensed a greater deference and respect from him than was evident before. "Lieutenant, can I talk with you for a minute or two?" He glanced tentatively at me, then down at the floor. He added, "But I understand if you're too busy...." I could tell he expected me to say no.

"Of course," I replied, gesturing at my apartment with a guilty laugh, "if you can stand the mess. You can see I've got my belongings strewn everywhere. But I think we can find room to sit." Red breathed a deep sigh of relief, then sat down stiffly on one end of the sofa, his hands clasped together in his lap. As I sat opposite him in an easy chair, he looked me directly in the eyes. "Lieutenant, may I be completely frank with you?"

"Certainly."

"I told you I came here directly from prison. What I didn't say was that I was sent there for murder. That was 15 years ago." He hesitated to check my reaction. I nodded understandingly. Though I felt there was little these men could say that would startle me, what came next took me completely aback. "Well, I'm about to tell you something only a few people know, and they're sworn to secrecy. While I was serving my time, I killed two more men. I killed them with a shiv I made from a razor blade." He paused again to study my face. He spoke so bluntly and with such little inflection that I was startled—and I'm sure my surprise showed.

What kind of a man is this sitting across from me? I wondered. *What kind of a man could do the things he says he did and speak of them so impassively? Does he have no conscience?*

Then, abruptly, almost as if he were reading my mind, Red dropped his guard; the stolid expression on his face gave way, and he broke into deep sobs, his big shoulders heaving. Impulsively, I moved over next to him and embraced him, holding him close. I was awed at my own behavior, but it came naturally to me—almost like a reflex. And I did not regret it.

"But the thing that scares me the most," he added between sobs, his chin upon my shoulder, "is that while I was there in prison, one day in a fit of rage I blasphemed the Holy Spirit. I committed the unpardonable sin! Now there's no forgiveness that God can give me." He looked up into my face. "Lieutenant, I've got emphysema. The doctor tells me I don't have much time! Is there no hope for heaven for a man like me?"

Stunned at the dramatic contrast between the man's earlier indifference and his present outburst, I held him tightly in my arms. He reciprocated, clutching me closer to him. I rocked back and forth with him as if he were a child. I saw us as two souls clasped together. I couldn't begin to understand the man, for he had been down roads I could never imagine. But I knew intuitively that he was sincerely terrified and also that God dearly loved him. And since God loved him, so must I.

Pondering how to respond, I gathered my thoughts. I studied Red's face and I could now see indications of emphysema—the shortness of breath, the audible breathing. While the symptoms were not prominent, now that I knew what to look for, they were unmistakable.

"Red, I want to address your concerns about what Scripture calls the unforgivable sin," I told him.

Tears still issuing from his eyes, he lifted his head, studying my face, hoping against all hope. I was becoming more and more awed at the immense responsibility God had given me, that trust that came with Salvation Army officership. I was intrigued and amazed that this big man looked up to me so, searching for the mind of God in the words of such a new Christian as I.

I consciously fought against any tendency toward condescension or disdain that may be surfacing in me. Although Red's confession of multiple murders greatly repulsed me, I reminded myself again that God still loved him, in fact he loved him no less than he loved me, despite what Red had done (Matt. 5:43-48). Patiently, I rose from the sofa, sat down opposite him, and handed him a handkerchief. I struggled to reconcile in my mind his portrayal of himself as a multiple killer with the image of the man who sat across from me, a humble man terrified that God may not forgive him.

Looking him directly in the eyes, I said, "Red, first of all I want to assure you that God loves you very, very much. And he will never cease loving you. Your confession shocks me—your confession of murder, even multiple murders—but if you have a complete change of heart, I assure you that God will forgive you even that.

"This topic of the unpardonable sin is one in which I have had an interest. And the true meaning cannot contradict Scripture. Looking at Scripture as a whole, I have concluded that the only sin God will not forgive is permanently rejecting Christ with such finality that no future repentance is possible. This and only this is the sin against the Holy Spirit—the unpardonable sin mentioned in Scripture. I am not alone in this interpretation; many students of the Bible agree. A person does not commit an unpardonable sin by simply reciting certain words. Rather, it is committed by developing a heart so hard that he turns his back on God, permanently rejecting God's offer of love and forgiveness. Your very behavior tells me that you are repentant today. Am I correct? Do you truly repent of your past sins? Are you truly sorry for the wrong you've done against both God and man? And are you sorry enough to quit? To completely change your life?"

"Yes! Yes!" he announced emphatically. "I am so very sorry! I love the Lord! I just don't know if he can forgive me, I mean a man like me. Just look at the wrong I've done!"

I opened my Bible to Isaiah and read: *"Let the wicked forsake his way and the evil man his thoughts. Let him turn to the Lord, and he will have mercy on him, and to our God, for he will freely pardon"* (55:7 NIV).

I told Red the story of the prodigal son and pointed out that the son's father was "filled with compassion" for his returning son. I explained how even King David committed murder, but God had forgiven him. I read Psalm 51, stressing verses 14 and 17 where David prays: *Save me from bloodguilt, O God, the God who saves me, and my tongue will sing of your righteousness…. The sacrifices of God are a broken spirit; a broken and contrite heart, O God, you will not despise* (NIV).

I asked Red if he would pray with me, and he readily agreed. Together we got down on our knees upon the floor, and I held his hands as he gave his heart to Jesus Christ. The regret was so evident in the man. As I led him in reciting the sinner's prayer, his lips quivered—he was so moved.

"Dear Father God in heaven, I come to you in the name of Jesus. I acknowledge to you that I am a sinner, and I am sorry for my sins and the life that I have lived. I need your forgiveness."

Glancing at me as he finished, Red's eyes were wet, but his face was aglow with joy and relief; it was as if a mountain of guilt was now removed from his shoulders. At that moment, despite the significant differences between us, I identified completely with him. Though the specifics of his past life differed greatly from mine, there were two very basic things we had in common: we had both been burdened by tremendous guilt—we were broken men—and we had both finally found release through humbling ourselves, stepping away from dependence upon our own strength, and accepting Christ's offer to give over our burdens to him. I read to him: *But you, O Sovereign Lord, deal well with me for your name's sake; out of the goodness of your love, deliver me. For I am poor and needy, and my heart is wounded within me* (Ps. 109:21-22 NIV).

Red stood and, just before departing, grasped me tightly around the waist in a last, large bearhug. "Thank you, Lieutenant. Thank you so much," he said.

"It is my pleasure, Red! God bless you." I replied.

"God bless you," he replied, embarrassingly wiping away another tear as he gently closed the door.

For the longest time I sat back in the easy chair, reliving the experience, marveling at the wonderful love and power of God. The full potential of the ministry to which he had called me was slowly sinking in. I closed my eyes and prayed aloud a profound prayer of thanksgiving to God for making use of me as an instrument of his will. "Thank you, dear Lord! Thank you!" I murmured.

BIBLE SELECTION

Have mercy on me, O God,
according to your unfailing love;
according to your great compassion
blot out my transgressions.
Wash away all my iniquity
and cleanse me from my sin.

For I know my transgressions,
and my sin is always before me.
Against you, you only, have I sinned
and done what is evil in your sight,
so that you are proved right when you speak
and justified when you judge.
Surely I was sinful at birth,
sinful from the time my mother conceived me.
Surely you desire truth in the inner parts;
you teach me wisdom in the inmost place.

Cleanse me with hyssop, and I will be clean;
wash me and I will be whiter than snow (Ps. 51:1-7 NIV).

REFLECTION _____

The experience with Red was deeply humbling, for I knew I was dealing with things far beyond my ability to fathom: the mind and the soul of a killer. I could not begin to grasp the workings of such a mind. What must it be like to kill a man, to feel the knife in your hand slip into the body of another person? What must it be like to see the person you knifed fall to the floor lifeless at your feet? How can one live with himself afterward? Yet here was such a man, sitting, talking dispassionately with me about such deeds. Then in the next moment he bursts into tears, deathly worried about his soul, sobbing like a small child in my arms. He was terrified at the thought of what the next world may bring. Here were matters with which only God could deal.

But I had no doubt that the God who contrived and created our stunning world could change the heart of even such a man as this. At the very moment I held him in my arms, I knew beyond any shadow of a doubt that God would not shrug him off. *[God] is patient with you, not wanting anyone to perish, but everyone to come to repentance* (2 Pe. 3:9 NIV).

Dear Lord, thank you so much for empowering me to love this man who came begging for your pardon. What a tremendous responsibility you have given me—to hold a man's soul in my hands! You enabled me to briefly see into a life utterly alien from my own and feel something of your love for even him.

Dear God, I freely admit that I can't begin to fathom how a man could commit murder, yet I know that I am no judge of such things, and I thank you for freeing me from that responsibility (James 4:12).

In the precious name of Jesus Christ my Savior I pray. Amen.

CHAPTER TWENTY-FOUR

A New Kind of Survivor Guilt

A HORN BLARED BEHIND me, startling me where I was parked at the intersection. It blared again, and this time I heard my name called. Glancing over my shoulder, I spotted, one lane over and two cars back, a driver's arm waving aloft with four fingers held out. "Four years! Major Doss! Four years clean and sober!" a man called. Laughing, I waved back. I did not recognize the man or the voice, but I knew what he was telling me. An ARC graduate, he was letting me know he was still clean and sober three and one half years after completing our six-month alcohol and drug rehab program. I recalled neither his name nor his face, but he remembered me.

There are many joys that come from running an ARC program. I think about the young man who called me in Anaheim, California, to invite me to his college graduation from a university in Colorado. This was three years after he graduated from an ARC program I had run in Denver. There are so many victories, so many success stories, although we never hear again from many of our graduates who do well and get on with their lives.

Then there are those who keep you awake nights, whose faces haunt you down through the years. Faces of those who not only relapsed but died in their addictions. They haunt me, I think, for the same reason I am haunted by the faces of many of my long-dead comrades from the Vietnam War. It's the wondering if there was something I could have done differently that may have saved them. And why them and not me? Henry Warner was such a man.

Early on in my Salvation Army career I remarried, and my bride Mary and I were sent to assist another officer in charge of a large ARC program. It was there that I met Henry, a 50-year-old man with a drinking problem that had dogged him since his teens. During work breaks I often sat and talked with him as he puffed on his Marlboro cigarettes. Not intimidated by my uniform, he used me as a sounding board. He vented for hours. Of course I was aware that many of his stories were tall tales, but eventually he moved from the realm of fantasy to that of realism, from braggadocio to somber reality. He talked of his Vietnam War service (we had this in common—he saw me as a comrade in arms), of his two failed marriages (I was also divorced) and an adult daughter in San Francisco who had refused for years to talk to him. He spoke longingly about how much he missed her, how he would dearly love to see her just one more time.

One of the reasons I took such a liking to Henry, I think, is that we had much in common—though certainly not all. But I also wanted desperately to "save him" from his habit. During his many years of bumming around the country, he had never been able to put more than nine months of sobriety together at one time. I also wanted desperately to facilitate his conversion, to show him that through leaning on Jesus Christ as his Higher Power, it would be possible for him to achieve the sobriety and peace of mind he so desperately sought—and to save his soul.

Then one Sunday morning, following my worship service message, after praying for God to work in the souls of the unsaved among us, I opened my eyes to see Henry kneeling at the altar. My heart leaped for joy, and I hastily made my way down from the platform to his side.

"Would you like me to pray with you, Henry?"

"Yes, please," he murmured, his eyes closed in prayer.

I prayed for God to work mightily in his heart, to give Henry the strength and wisdom he needed to remain clean and sober one day at a time. I prayed that he would learn to lean daily on God's power for this strength. I reminded Henry of the words of 1 John 1:9, *If we confess our sins, he is faithful and just and will forgive us our sins and purify us from all unrighteousness* (NIV); then I led him in a profound, sincere prayer of confession. When all was said and done, Henry stood and I gave him a huge bearhug, hesitant to ever let him go, and he hugged me in return. "Thank you, Lieutenant, thank you," he said over and over again.

Over the days that followed, I worked closely with him, chatting with him daily, joking and praying with him. And I believe I applauded harder than anybody else when he was presented his certificate of completion in the chapel graduation ceremony, as he held it aloft for all to see.

The very next day, however, the men's residence manager gave notice, and the administrator pulled me aside. "I'm going to offer the job to Henry," he said.

"What? Residence management is a very stressful job. I don't think Henry's ready for it; his sobriety is tenuous at best."

"I disagree," he responded. "He's working a good program, attending 12-step meetings regularly. Have you noticed the way the other men look up to him? They really respect him. That's what I need in a residence manager."

I shook my head. "No," I insisted. "Don't do this. He has never put nine months of sobriety together before. And he's got just six now. He's not strong enough."

The officer looked me directly in the eye. "He's all I've got," he said and walked away.

My heart sank. I walked out to the warehouse where Henry was assisting the shipping supervisor to load a truck of donated goods for transport to one of our thrift stores. Although he had graduated the night before, Henry had not yet checked out. The men were permitted to stay on for a few weeks until they found a job. In Henry's case, it appeared the job had found him. He spotted me and grinned broadly.

"That was some night last night, huh, Lieutenant?"

"Sure was, Henry! How are you this morning?"

"Good!" he said, with a broad grin. "Couldn't be better!"

I didn't know what to say to him. I could not countermand the administrator's decision, and subterfuge was not my way. "Will you have a few minutes after you knock off?" I asked. He nodded. "Can you stop by my office then?"

"Sure thing!" he replied, grinning.

A couple of hours later, as the warehouse doors were closing, I sat in my office chair, staring at a hole in the wall. I had been praying fervently for Henry. I was worried.

As he entered, he was grinning from ear to ear. Five-foot-ten, with thinning light hair and numerous facial wrinkles from a lifetime of smoking cigarettes, Henry was nevertheless lit up like a Christmas tree. I knew instantly that he had already been offered the job. "I'm going to be the new residence manager!" he announced.

My face dropped. "I know," I said. "Would you mind sitting down, Henry? I would like to talk to you about that."

After he sat down, I pulled my chair over next to his and looked him directly in the eyes. "Are you ready for this?" I asked pointedly.

For a moment, I thought I saw a flicker of doubt in his face, but he immediately regained his composure. "Yes. Yes, I am."

"You're sure? Because this arrangement can be undone just like that." I snapped my fingers for emphasis. "It will be as if you were never offered the position. There are many jobs out there besides this one. I know that managing this residence of 150 men can be very stressful. It's particularly hard on someone new in recovery. You live in the building; the men can be argumentative and stubborn; a crisis at night will interrupt your sleep. I don't want you to relapse, Henry. I love you, man!" I emphasized the last two sentences; I meant them. I had recently done a funeral for one of the men who relapsed—who overdosed—and I didn't want to do another so soon, especially for someone whom I had come to know and like as well as Henry.

He stood, reached out, and placed both hands on my shoulders, then looked me in the eyes appreciatively and smiled. "I know you care, Lieutenant. And I appreciate it very much. But I've got this under control. I'm working a good Alcoholics Anonymous program; I know I'll be okay. I can do this job!"

"It's your decision to make, of course," I answered, "but may I pray with you?"

I stood. Holding his hands in mine, I prayed hard for Henry, that he would be attentive to his devotional duties, turning to the Lord for wisdom, listening to God's guidance and heeding it, that he would lean on the Lord for power and remain humble before the demon of alcoholism. I prayed for the Lord to place a shield of protection around him, protecting him from the devil's onslaught. After we prayed, he gave me a big bearhug. He left a bit teary-eyed but still on cloud nine from the job offer. Me? I continued praying for him as well as for all the other men in the program, who were stalked daily by the demon of addiction. And I prayed for myself.

Henry immediately took charge of a house that was still reeling from the relapse of its most recent manager, also a program graduate. Bill, the assistant manager, had been doing his best to hold down the fort with the support of a couple of men still in the program who were assigned work therapy positions in the residence. While a good, steady guy and very dependable—a good number two—Bill lacked the leadership traits needed to effectively do the manager's job. He was gruff and snapped at the men too quickly, especially when he was tired.

Bill had recently been doing both his own job and the manager's. He was struggling and stressed and was clearly quite relieved when Henry was given the position. The two appeared to immediately hit it off.

Over the days that followed, I watched closely as Henry moved into the role of manager. Working hand in hand with Bill, he pulled the reins gradually tighter until the place eventually seemed to run like clockwork. During the graduation ceremonies of the next few weeks, I listened attentively as Henry, in his role of residence manager, opened the ceremony with congratulatory remarks for the new graduates and then, as was the custom, led the house in a recitation of the Serenity Prayer: "God grant me the serenity to accept the things I cannot change, courage to change the things I can, and the wisdom to know the difference."

It was clear from the way the men responded to him that Henry had won their allegiance. And he showed no signs of stress. Over the months that followed, Henry seemed to grow even more into the role, and I thanked God.

Ten months after Henry became residence manager, the ARC bustled with even more activity than usual as the department heads prepared for the annual review. The ARC commander and his support staff would spend three days going over every aspect of the center's operation. Along with the clinical director, Henry oversaw the preparation of the residence. Everyone put in long hours, working hard to spruce up the place. When the big day finally arrived, Henry stood by proud and tall as the ARC commander and his staff looked into every corner of the residence.

At the wrap-up meeting, Henry beamed with pride as the commander praised the appearance of the facility. He also commended Henry, along with the other program staff, for the order and discipline that was apparent in the behavior of the men. I, too, was happy for Henry.

However, a few weeks later, the dreaded telltale signs of relapse began to appear. The first thing I noticed was the increasing sloppiness of Henry's appearance. While his grooming was never the sharpest, he had always shaved each morning, kept a neat haircut and wore clean and pressed attire. Almost overnight, it became evident that he was skipping shaving and bathing. His hair was in disarray in the morning and his clothes were wrinkled.

My habit was to make a round of the warehouse at 5:30 a.m. to ensure that the dock supervisor was getting everything ready for the 6 a.m. crew to unload the trucks filled with donations picked up the day before. By 6 a.m. I was at the residence front desk to check in with the folks there. I had always been pleased to find Henry making his morning rounds promptly, greeting me with a bright smile. This was now happening less and less as Henry dragged in later and later. My heart sank. It was just as I feared. I knew he was drinking.

When I pulled Henry aside and questioned him, his reaction was like that of so many men I had seen relapse—blatant denial. Gone was the bright smile and confident demeanor I had come to love. Gone was the charismatic leader of men that we had so admired. His eyes were evasive though his manner direct as he invented excuse after excuse to explain his tardiness and decreasing efficiency. He swallowed mints like candy in an effort to hide the odor of alcohol on his breath. Somehow, though, he managed to evade blowing positive on the breathalyzer, making it difficult for us to validate his drinking. And he was careful not to drink on duty. Henry was carefully timing his drinking to fall within the acceptable limit of the range on the breathalyzer.

I counseled him—and documented it in writing—for three weeks while the men in the residence grew more and more frustrated and Bill, the dependable assistant manager, sadly watched his new boss go the way of the former one. It was a very distressing state of affairs. I felt like a failure myself.

Try as I would, I could not get Henry's attention. The drinking escalated rapidly and his performance deteriorated accordingly. Finally, three weeks after the first signs appeared, I called him into my office and explained I had no choice but to fire him. I did so as kindly as I could, trying to coax him into entering another rehab program across town. In fact, I had already called and arranged it, but Henry would have none of it. Defiant in his outrage and anger, this "stranger" heaped verbal abuse upon me. I watched him pityingly, then escorted him to his room to get the building keys from him.

I was surprised to find that he had already packed; he had evidently seen the writing on the wall. Handing me the keys, he looked at me—this 50-year-old man who looked 65, unshaven, gray hair in disarray—and for the first time since he had begun drinking again, I saw hurt in his eyes. For a moment I thought I was going to hear some words of remorse, but it was not to be. Instead, he emitted a four-letter epithet, then promptly knelt and retrieved from beneath his bed a jug of bourbon wrapped in a brown paper bag. I was shocked at this show of bravado! With a suitcase in one hand and the jug in the other, Henry strode out of the room and through the front door.

"Take care, Henry! Be careful! Remember, call me if you need my help getting into treatment!"

"I won't forget you, Lieutenant! Sorry it had to end like this," he called back to me as he took a swig from the bottle. I watched him walk along the sidewalk until he disappeared from sight.

Dear God, take care of Henry, I prayed. *Dear Lord, please take care of him.*

I didn't hear from him again for quite a while and thought I may never, that Henry would be just one more relapse statistic whose ultimate outcome I would never know. I prayed for him daily, as I did for other men who had fallen off the wagon or relapsed on cocaine, heroin or methamphetamines.

We were fortunate to fill the residence manager position with a man with three years of sobriety who appeared to be working an excellent 12-step program and had solid managerial experience behind him. But just two months after I watched the back of Henry's lanky form walk out of sight into the city, I received a call from a nurse on the detox ward of a local hospital. Henry was a patient there, she told me. He was out of his head, going through the DTs. She explained that a police patrol had come upon him passed out on the street and had brought him there. She had found an employee identification tag with our phone number and thought he might still be employed with us. She wanted to know if he had health coverage. Listening to her, my heart sank, but I also thought: *At least he's alive! Maybe there's still a chance that he will regain sobriety and keep it.*

A few hours later, Mary and I entered the hospital ward to spot a man on a cot across the room shaking violently. I stopped stock-still, staring, spell-bound by what I saw. Henry was strapped to his cot, raging, jerking, straining with all his might against the straps that bound him. His face was bruised, skinned and battered. His legs, feet and hands trembled spasmodically. I saw a madman suffering horribly, screaming out like an animal in his misery. Repeatedly his head spun rapidly—left, right, forward, then to the left and right again.

As I approached, I called out to Henry, but he didn't acknowledge me. He looked directly at us, yet there was absolutely no hint of recognition upon his face. It was as if he were completely blind. This was Henry alright, but not the Henry we knew and remembered. Yet it was still the Henry I loved. For a moment I saw in my mind's eye the man he had been—the cheery, confident, laughing man, thirsty to know a brighter, better way, ever full of questions. I recalled the excitement (and poorly concealed doubts) he displayed upon being hired. I remembered the charismatic leader of men and the in-charge manner that he originally displayed in the job.

What went wrong? Why did he begin drinking again? The answer was there, staring me in the face. Henry was an alcoholic; he wasn't ready for such a stressful job. How often have I heard those words! And how often have I said them myself!

Then I recalled something that another graduate said had come to his mind on his first day in our program as he sat in the chapel, gazing up at the cross above the platform: "I realized that Christ died for a suffering alcoholic like me."

Dear God, help Henry, I prayed. *I know you died for all the suffering people of the world. I know you love him dearly.* As I watched Henry gyrate insensibly against the straps that bound him, I saw myself lying there, bound with those same straps, howling and pulling against them with all my might—and my heart went out to Henry! I suffered there with him in that ward. Closing my eyes, my face bowed, I prayed aloud for him, for God to give him peace.

Five days later, I stood again by Henry's bunk, and a sheepishly smiling, composed man apologized to me after I told him my wife and I had been out to see him earlier. His face still showed the bruises and scratches, but he was now shaven and his hair neatly combed. "I don't remember you being here—honest, I don't. I must have been a sight for sore eyes!"

"That you were!" I exclaimed good-naturedly. "I felt for you going through that turmoil. But it's so good to see you in your right mind today! We've missed you, Henry, since you left. What was it like for you out there?"

"Terrible. It was terrible, Lieutenant. Much worse than it has ever been before. I really thought I was going to die out there this time. I remember crawling on all fours along the street, in the pouring rain, my elbows and knees scraped and bleeding. I'll die if I go through this again! I'm too old. This was my last run! I'm done!"

I nodded. I understood. "But praise God you're alive and safe today. You have another opportunity to get clean and sober—and remain that way. So, what's the next step? What do you intend to do after leaving here?"

He paused, looked me directly in the face, then scanned the room, looking at the other patients lying in their cots or sitting up, talking with visitors; then he glanced down at the floor. Decisively, he turned to me. "I would like to go back through the program, that same one. Yes, I would like to start over—right there in that residence that I ran for three months."

Alarm bells went off in my head! It was rare for men to request to reenter a program where they had recently been supervisors, especially while there were still men there who remembered them. They found the prospect too humiliating. "Are you sure?" I asked him. "There are other programs in town."

"I want to. I want to start over," he said. "This is something I need to do."

I pulled up a chair and talked at length with him about what he would do differently when working the new recovery program, what his new plan would be. At the conclusion of the visit I prayed with him, sitting by his bed, my hand on his shoulder. He announced his intention, when he checked out of the hospital the following Wednesday afternoon, to go directly to our facility and check in by 2 p.m. He had a ride, he said. It was all set up. I left the hospital with a good feeling. Henry had a chance.

But Wednesday 2 p.m. came and went, and there was no Henry. My heart sank once again. Where was he? The next morning I called the hospital ward; they confirmed that he had checked out as scheduled. It was the following Saturday morning that I received the fateful call. I remember it like it was yesterday—the shock, the astonishment I felt, the sinking feeling in the pit of my stomach that settled there and would not go away. The caller was the pastor of the local Presbyterian church. His words hit me like a ton of bricks. "Henry is dead," he said, then asked if I would like to perform a memorial service for him at the church. I listened to the pastor's account with difficulty; it was all I could do to hold the phone to my ear. I took his name and number and told him I would call him back. I hung up the phone and stared down at my desk silently for the longest time. Tears mounted in my eyes.

The minister explained that after checking out of the hospital, Henry had stopped at a liquor store, then got an overnight room at a nearby cheap hotel. During the night, a smoke alarm went off; the fire department responded and discovered Henry's bed smoldering. They determined that he probably had passed out from the alcohol and the ashes from a cigarette he was smoking had caught the bed linens on fire. Although his body was badly burned, it was smoke inhalation that killed him.

When signing in, Henry had given the minister as a reference, and he was called. Later, I learned that Henry had worked for him briefly as a custodian after leaving our employment. Over the few weeks Henry worked there, before the alcoholism ended that job as well, he had talked with the minister about his affiliation with The Salvation Army, about me, and about his many friends in the ARC program. So the minister decided to call me when he got the terrible news.

As these men die one after another, I thought, *a little of me dies with them. It's like Vietnam all over again, the survivor guilt—why them and not me?* But since Christ came into my heart, I have an answer for the enigmas, the incomprehensible questions of life. As Kierkegaard wrote, "Everything is possible spiritually speaking, but in the finite world there is much that is not possible."[16]

Therefore through Christ I have an answer now: once I am resigned to my own finiteness, I can give my burden over to him for whom all things are possible (Matt. 19:26). I need not be destroyed; rather, empowered by God, I can walk these death journeys with these men, make a difference, and come out the other side still useful to my God. To the degree I am invested in these men's lives, I am invested in my own, and strengthened thereby. Therefore, although it hurts a great deal when I see one die, I can pick myself up and get back to the work Christ has for me.

There would be no more chances this side of glory for Henry to get clean and sober. At the midweek worship service, I announced the news to the men. When I gave them an opportunity to share a remembrance of Henry, arm after arm shot up. There were many spontaneous, touching accounts of the goodness of the man, of the compassionate deeds he had done for them. But there were also several questions. One was: "Lieutenant, is it possible that Henry is in heaven?" You could have heard a pin drop, for unspoken was another question: "Can a person who died while intoxicated be accepted into heaven?" In our Bible studies I had shared the following Scripture from Galatians: *The acts of the sinful nature are obvious: sexual immorality, impurity and debauchery; idolatry and witchcraft; hatred, discord, jealousy, fits of rage, selfish ambition, dissensions, factions and envy; drunkenness, orgies, and the like. I warn you, as I did before, that those who live like this will not inherit the kingdom of God* (5:19-21 NIV).

I responded to the men's questions by quoting 1 John 1:9, *If we confess our sins, he is faithful and just and will forgive us our sins and purify us from all unrighteousness* (NIV) and informed them that I witnessed Henry's confession of faith in that very chapel. I reminded them of their own testimonies of Henry's good deeds, of the love he showed for them and others. I spoke at length of the grace and love of God, reciting from Ephesians:

> *And I pray that you, being rooted and established in love, may have power, together with all the saints, to grasp how wide and long and high and deep is the love of Christ, and to know this love that surpasses knowledge—that you may be filled to the measure of all the fullness of God. Now to him who is able to do immeasurably more than all we ask or imagine, according to his power that is at work within us, to him be glory in the church and in Christ Jesus throughout all generations, for ever and ever! Amen* (3:17-21 NIV).

I reminded them that in the passage in Galatians 5, on the same par with drunkenness appear traits like jealousy, selfish ambition and envy. I pointed out to the men that the phrase "live like this," or "do such things" as it is rendered in some other translations is very broad. I advised them: "Therefore let us leave these deeper judgments in God's hands. In fact, he tells us: *'Do not judge, and you will not be judged. Do not condemn, and you will not be condemned. Forgive, and you will be forgiven'*" (Luke 6:37 NIV).

"I have no answer for your question," I said to the men. "That decision is God's to make. But I feel Henry is in heaven, for I knew the heart of the man. As many of you can verify, his was a heart of gold."

I led them in prayers of thanksgiving for the life of Henry. Many prayed from the bottom of their hearts. At the conclusion, I invited all who wished to attend to the memorial service for Henry at the Presbyterian church.

Over the days that followed, I searched high and low in vain for information on Henry's family. He had often spoken of an adult daughter in San Francisco. But no one knew any more than this, and try as I might, I could not locate her.

Consequently, when the date for the memorial service came around, there were no family members present. But there were several members of Henry's extended family—that is, the men and women from the 12-step community, an urban subculture comprised of many who knew him from the fellowship of Alcoholics Anonymous. Much of the ARC population showed up. Once again, following hymns and a devotional, I threw the floor open for people to give testimony, and person after person rose to tell how Henry had impacted their lives in a positive way. The accolades went on and on. And I shared from my heart of my deep love for him, for I knew a piece of my own heart had left this world.

BIBLE SELECTION _____

My conscience is clear, but that isn't what matters. It is the Lord himself who will examine me and decide. So be careful not to jump to conclusions before the Lord returns as to whether or not someone is faithful. When the Lord comes, he will bring our deepest secrets to light and will reveal our private motives. And then God will give to everyone whatever praise is due (1 Cor. 4:4-5 NLT).

REFLECTION _____

I have no idea what bearing Henry's heredity or early upbringing had on the man that he became; only God does. If mine were the same, perhaps I would have been strapped to a cot, raving like a madman, as well. Therefore, I will not judge Henry. I leave that to the Lord. He has the wisdom and insight to judge; I do not.

I knew three Henrys. First, the clean and sober man with the kind heart who had six months and more of sobriety behind him, the self-disciplined, efficient leader of men. Then there was the chronic alcoholic whose primary concern was where to get the next drink; this was the man I fired, the man I observed as he matter-of-factly retrieved the bottle of liquor from beneath his bed on his way out of the facility. The third Henry was the madman going through the DTs, screaming, shaking violently against the straps of the hospital cot, oblivious to all around him. I loved all three Henrys, none more than another, for they all were part and parcel of the same man. Did God love one more than the other? No, he loves with a deep, unconditional love that sees past the surface to the heart beneath (1 Sam. 16:7).

As the men from the rehab center stood and gave testimony to how Henry had touched their lives both as a friend and as residence manager, in the back of their minds they knew their fate might ultimately be like his—or it may not, depending on the life choices they made. They too saw a part of themselves in Henry.

But I thank God that he intervenes! For all the Henrys I have seen—addicts and alcoholics who die in their addiction—there are also many Joes and Jims and Bettys and Janes who get clean and sober and remain that way by relying on God's grace and love! I have seen them, too, but still it is the Henrys who dominate my thinking, who haunt me over the years. I want to save them all!

Dear Lord, forgive me if any decisions I made, words I said, or actions I performed contributed to the premature death of Henry. At this minute, Lord, I turn over to you my lingering guilt for my friends who died long ago in Vietnam fighting a war they did not understand. And for friends who died on the streets of Seattle, Denver, Los Angeles and other cities from the substance abuse they were unable to conquer. You loved them as much as I did, Lord, yet with a deeper, fuller love than I could ever know or express. I give over to you my guilt feelings this day.

Lord, I pray for all the Henrys out there, the men and women devastated by the disease of addiction. As you put people like me in their paths, dear Lord, grant us wisdom and strength and perseverance to do and say the right thing.

In the precious name of Jesus Christ my Savior I pray. Amen.

CHAPTER TWENTY-FIVE

Finally Set Free

JORDAN BISHOP WAS ONE of the first people I saw upon reporting to my new assignment as the ARC administrator. I had already been notified that he was the kitchen supervisor and a graduate of the rehab program from five years before. Spotting him as I entered the dining room, I tried to get a fix on the man. With dark brown skin and an afro (not completely masked by his head cover), Jordan made anything but a good first impression upon me. I frowned as I studied him from across the room. He was absorbed in his work, oblivious of me. It was just before lunch, and he was checking to see that everything was in order before the men and women stormed into the residence after a busy morning in the warehouse.

Then, as Jordan tilted his head slightly toward me, my stomach turned in disgust at what I saw: a gold-capped front tooth! *Who is this man who is now working for me?* I asked myself, with a shiver up and down my spine. *From what slum culture did he emerge?* And in my heart of hearts I immediately judged the man as unfit to hold the position he held. Yet, simultaneously, I kicked myself, asking: *Who am I, a mere human being, to judge this man who, like me, is a child of God?*

It was 1995. I accepted Christ as my Savior nine years before. At that time, God had begun the process of molding me. And I felt I had come far. Yet at moments like this I was shockingly reminded that I still struggled with my lifelong bias against African-Americans.

As I strode down between the dining room tables, Jordan spotted me and flashed a broad smile that showed off not one, but two, glittering gold-capped central incisors! As he stepped from behind the counter, I smartly held out a hand to him, trying my best to hide my gut-level disgust. I sensed it showed, but he appeared oblivious as he introduced himself.

"So you're Jordan Bishop," I replied. "I hear you're good at what you do."

"I try," Jordan said smoothly. "But I'm going to school. This job is fine for now, and I enjoy it, but I hope to be a minister someday. That's where God is calling me. I'm close to a bachelor of divinity degree now. However, I really love cooking and working with the beneficiaries here—giving back what God has given me."

Much of this was surprising news. I was impressed. My feelings of disgust mellowed slightly as I digested his softly spoken words, delivered with a metropolitan polish. But I found myself still frowning.

"That's quite an accomplishment," I replied. "And you've done that all in just five years while working full-time?" He nodded as I followed him into the kitchen, where I found everything clean and in its right place. I greeted the beneficiaries working hard at their duties and noticed how they deferred to Jordan respectfully. The relationship between them seemed to work well. I approved.

Over the weeks that followed, I was pleased at the feedback I received from the men on what an encouraging mentor Jordan was. I learned that he incorporated devotions into each morning break: a reading from the Bible and prayer. And Jordan was always ready to pray with the men over issues with which they were struggling. He was much more than a traditional work therapy supervisor.

At the same time, I was advertising for a chaplain—a position unfilled when I arrived. But I was stymied in my efforts. While interviewing applicants, I discovered I was unable to afford the salaries the best qualified candidates demanded. Days turned into weeks, and I worried about the men and women in my charge. Then one day I came to work to find an application for the position in my inbox from Jordan, together with a copy of his brand new bachelor of divinity degree certificate. As I reviewed the documents, I found myself conflicted; it had never occurred to me to hire a black person for the position. For one thing, I told myself, only 10 percent of our beneficiary population was black.

I put his application aside, telling myself Jordan was unqualified. Then a week later, I reported to work to find a beaming Jordan Bishop waiting for me at the front door of my office. Taken aback, I stood silently as he handed me a document showing he had been ordained as a minister by the church where he was currently serving as a deacon. He announced with some assurance: "Major Doss, does this help shore up my qualifications for the position of chaplain? I would really love the opportunity."

Within my mind a thousand thoughts jostled for dominance. The face of my boyhood friend Billy floated before me, followed by the image of old Willie Brown, who always called me "Sir." There was also the face of Jimmy Sparks, jaws clenched tight in anger. I was fighting a losing battle with my own soul. *God help me,* I prayed silently, my lips unmoving. *Help me understand what to do.* Finally, I asked Jordan to step into my office.

"Sit down, Jordan," I said to him, with a great sigh. "Tell me why you want this position and why you feel I should offer it to you." He followed me in, smiling from ear to ear. Another person might be pleased by Jordan's eagerness, but all I could manage at that moment was a frown at the thought that this dark-skinned man with the afro—and especially the gold teeth, which stood out like the brightest star in a dark sky—should presume to present Christ to the men and women in my charge. The image was anathema to me.

As I listened to Jordan talk, I prayed silently, and slowly but surely a peace came over me. Gradually I acknowledged this man's unique qualifications: He had been one of these men—just five years before he had been in their shoes. Then Christ had touched him and taken him on a journey of transformation that had not only empowered him to say no to drugs and alcohol but brought him peace. He had shown he was capable, and his compassion for the beneficiaries was as evident as his eagerness for the position.

Suddenly I stood, held out my hand to him, and announced, "Jordan, the job is yours."

"Yippee!" he shouted so abruptly I jumped. He shook my hand so hard I had to jerk it away.

Over the following weeks he did not disappoint me as he plunged into his work. He continued the style of mentoring he had demonstrated with his men in the kitchen. Now working full-time from an office, Jordan met many a spiritual need.

Meanwhile God continued carving away at the prejudices long lingering in my mind—which sometimes seemed permanently branded into my skull! Trapped by my biases, I often reacted by reflex to others according to my prejudices, rather than considering how God would have me respond. But ultimately the power of the Holy Spirit will not be denied; God will have his way! *There is neither Jew nor Greek, slave nor free, male nor female, for you are all one in Christ Jesus* teaches the word of God (Gal. 3:28 NIV). The message of this powerful Scripture gradually made its way from my head to my heart.

Just as I was beginning to think I was making real headway spiritually, an event occurred that rocked the foundations of my neat little world. A 35-year-old white woman who had graduated from the ARC women's program at our previous appointment and later worked as women's house manager there, applied for the position of manager of the women's program at our current appointment. When my wife Mary received Sandra Kurtz's application, both she and I were pleased. We felt Sandra (who liked to be called "Sandy") would work out very well. A few weeks later we met her at the airport. Afterwards we laughed together over dinner as we rehashed old times and caught up on all that had transpired with mutual acquaintances. It was great fun.

Sandy soon settled into her apartment at the women's residence and slipped comfortably into the familiar role of house manager. All seemed smooth sailing until one morning, while making my rounds, I came upon her and Jordan laughing together in the parking lot in a way that instantly made my skin crawl. Sandy, who was a comely woman, had her hand on Jordan's arm in what appeared to me a far too familiar fashion. Once more I was painfully reminded of how far my character lay from that of Christ. My reaction was completely visceral; I had no say in it at all! The emotion seemed to originate in my gut and make its way upward as uncontrollable rage. My instinct was to rush out into the parking lot and verbally lash out at my two employees, to shout at them that a relationship was completely out of the question—because she was white and he was black! Of course I did nothing of the sort. All I could do was stand there and seethe; I was pure misery from head to toe. Finally I dropped my head and slunk away.

Over the succeeding days, my suspicions were confirmed. Meanwhile, I daily fought an internal tug of war, not unlike that described by Paul: *I don't really understand myself, for I want to do what is right, but I don't do it. Instead, I do what I hate* (Rom. 7:15 NLT).

Often as I stood talking with Jordan, Sandy by my wife's side, I could not miss the expression of adoration on Sandy's face, her eyes firmly fixed on Jordan. But rather than feeling happy for Sandy that she had found someone (as I probably would have been had the man been white), instead I felt deep resentment. *Is there no white man good enough for her?* I angrily asked myself. *Why must it be him? What's* wrong *with her?* But deep in my gut I knew it wasn't Sandy with the problem—it was me.

Soon the whole facility was talking about the budding relationship between Jordan and Sandy. Meanwhile I spent many an hour in my office, my Bible open before me, asking God to guide and enlighten me. Often I got down on my knees, for there was something about kneeling that seemed to help me better humble myself. Repeatedly I prayed: "Please, God, take this prejudice from me. I know from your Word and your Holy Spirit's conviction that there is no right place in my heart for such thoughts and emotions. Please, God, take them from me." And over the weeks that followed, I felt myself changing.

In time I spoke with both Jordan and Sandy, counseling them on caution in their relationship. God gave me the words and control to show objectivity, and both of them listened respectfully. I was making headway, but I was soon to be tested again.

Michael Stewart was a 38-year-old, fully bald black man who grew up on the streets of Los Angeles. He wound up at our ARC, far from his place of origin, while serving in the US Army. His boyhood gang attitudes and drug habit followed him and led to an unexpected discharge, but not before he attained a respectable NCO rank and acquired leadership skills. While in our ARC, Michael found the Lord and, after graduating, drove a truck for us for two years before he was promoted to dock foreman. There he continued to grow in his relationship with Christ and bloomed as he supervised the men in the warehouse. I liked Michael a lot and looked forward to my daily conversations with him as I made my rounds.

Imagine my surprise when, just months after Jordan and Sandy began dating, I spotted Michael being dropped off for work one morning by a white woman with two small children in the back seat. I watched him say goodbye to her in a very friendly fashion. But this time my reaction was far less visceral; though startled, my skin did not crawl, nor did I seethe with anger. Rather, I took the time to pray a silent prayer and was able to keep calm. It was as if I were watching myself from a distance, seeing God answer my prayers. As the days passed, I learned my surmise was correct: Michael was dating the woman. But I accepted it and thanked God for giving me a new heart.

In time, Jordan and Sandy went their separate ways. Michael, on the other hand, eventually married his new flame. Me? God continued to work on me. He continues to this day. His work in each of us is never done. Through his grace, I emerged from both incidents far more accepting of all people and with an even deeper love for God in my heart.

BIBLE SELECTION

When I was a child, I talked like a child, I thought like a child, I reasoned like a child. When I became a man, I put childish ways behind me (1 Cor. 13:11 NIV).

REFLECTION _____

More than 15 years have passed since I walked into that center dining hall, spied Jordan from a distance and judged him with a glance; more than a decade and a half since I spotted Sandy and him laughing together and instinctively seethed with rage. I stand amazed at how much God has changed my heart since then. Today, as a chaplain myself, I regularly counsel black men with white girlfriends or wives, who have children of mixed race, and think nothing of it. I praise God that today I see no color lines!

Still, I remain amazed that nine years after Jesus touched me in the cab of my car that summer night in San Diego, I remained viscerally attached to my past. Why did it take so long for me to be set free? I can only attribute this to the powerful hold our roots have on us—the grip of that which shapes us in our early, formative years. Only the Spirit of God can set us free of this.

Many of the men I counsel remain tortured by troubled childhoods; cruelty was branded into them. I stress to them that all of us must permit the Spirit of God to remove our inner fears, resentments and guilt feelings (which otherwise rule us) and replace them with his abundant love. Praise God—I finally did! The apostle Paul expressed my feelings so very well: *What a wretched man I am! Who will rescue me from this body of death? Thanks be to God—through Jesus Christ our Lord!* (Rom. 7:24-25 NIV). Thank you, Lord, for your bountiful love to me and to so many others!

In the precious name of Jesus Christ my Savior I pray. Amen.

CHAPTER TWENTY-SIX

Embracing the Victories

BRETT BRONSON CLEARLY HAD something on his mind. As I spoke with the men lingering after the Bible study, he paced just a few feet away, hands clasped tightly behind his back, gazing at the floor. This was my first opportunity to speak with the young man who had recently checked into our recovery program.

"Brett, I can see something's troubling you. How can I help you?"

"Major. I have a question. I didn't want to talk while the others were still around. It's this…."

Brett had a coarse, gravelly voice and a nervous demeanor. His hands flew rapidly this way and that as he scratched and rubbed his arms, neck and face as he talked. Brett was 34 years old and had been using cocaine for 15 years. This was his first rehab program. He was not court-mandated, but had checked himself in voluntarily. His question was a good one.

"Major, now that I'm permitted to have visitors, this woman I've been living with for several years wants to come see me; but she's still in her addiction, using drugs. I'm concerned how that will affect me, now that I've made up my mind to quit. What should I do?"

Brett's question was one I heard often from men and women in the program. Now that they were in rehab, they were confronted with a quandary—whether to continue to associate with family members and friends who were still active in their addictions. Our answer to such queries is always the same: no, they should break the tie until the other party becomes clean and sober as well. This was, however, a tough thing for many of them to do. Yet such was my response to Brett.

"I figured that's what you would say," he replied. "But it's hard to say no to her. She is so persistent."

Over the days that followed, I watched Brett closely and smiled to see him grow. Originally characterized by a coarse, suspicious personality, the roughness slowly smoothed out as he became more trusting. He eventually broke all ties with the woman. I was pleased. This by itself was evidence that Brett took his sobriety very seriously; he listened to what his advisors had to say.

Then one day, as I was walking by the warehouse, I heard him shout out: "Get your hands off me!" I spun about to see Brett and another beneficiary in a scuffle several yards away. A supervisor raced toward them and, by the time I arrived at the scene, each man was being restrained, though they continued to exchange epithets. The supervisor ordered them to cool it.

"What's going on here?" I demanded.

"Oh, they got into it, Major. I think they're over it now. Aren't you, men?"

"Yes. I'm fine," snapped Brett. Then, glancing guiltily at me, he added, "I'm sorry."

"Yeah, me too," said the other fellow. "It's okay."

Fighting was a very serious offense. The penalty was usually immediate termination from the program, and they both knew it. At the weekly case conference that afternoon the incident was discussed in depth and, since this was the first serious offense for both men and they had each expressed deep remorse, we decided to give them one last chance. Each, however, was given a 30-day restriction to the premises, termination of all visitation privileges, and intense homework assignments requiring them to ponder the cause and consequences of their actions. It was becoming more and more evident that Brett had a serious anger problem. I wasn't at all sure he was going to make it over the long haul.

Issues of interpersonal conflict continued to plague his stay in the program, but he held on, though by a thin margin. His work therapy supervisor, Steve Johnson, had faith in him and went to bat for him at every opportunity. "Brett is getting it. He's growing," Steve said. "He's got some rough edges, so it will take him a while, but he is very serious about his sobriety, about getting his life together. I have faith he will make it if he just hangs in there."

About 90 days into the six-month program, Brett showed up at my breakfast Bible study for the first time. This voluntary early morning study, attended by a dozen or so men, met for an hour each weekday morning at 6 a.m. I led them in open discussions about a passage or selected passages of Scripture. I was careful to pick texts that spoke to where they were in their lives and whose study would hopefully strengthen them.

Brett listened, hanging on to every word. He knew very little about the Bible. Growing up unchurched, Christianity was a whole new world to him, but he was now eager to grasp all he could. And so I worked to tutor men like him, and at the same time keep those well-versed in Scripture enthused and challenged by the study. It was a struggle to balance both, but was well worth the effort to me.

Over coffee and orange juice, between bites of scrambled egg and toast, we discussed what the Scriptures had to say about anger and patience and prayer. We talked about the avenues by which we may harness God's power (Eph. 3:20) and the ways in which we can be open and receptive to his leading (Ps. 143:10). Brett listened carefully and sought to apply throughout his day what he learned in each morning's study.

Then one Sunday, as I concluded the message and commenced the altar call and person after person came forward, Brett caught my eye. He was clearly struggling. I walked over to him. "Brett, would you like to come forward and pray?"

He looked up at me, his eyes revealing a sincerity I had not seen before. "Will you pray with me, Major?"

"Absolutely," I responded.

Together we walked up to the altar and knelt, and I led him in the sinner's prayer. Then I prayed hard for his soul, his family, his continued sobriety, that he would grow up in the Lord one day at a time, leaning on him. Brett gave his soul to Jesus Christ. Another one for the kingdom!

And despite the tough times, Brett survived the six-month program. I vividly remember how joyful he was on his graduation day as his mother and sister looked on, just glowing; I have seen few things more beautiful than his mother's radiant face. A hard-working single parent, she had stayed close and was supportive to him throughout the duration of the program. Brett had not seen his father, an alcoholic, since he left the family when Brett was small. Brett asked his mom to take a photo of him and me together. And I have that moment captured to this day: there he is in a suit and tie, his left arm wrapped loosely about my waist, as he holds aloft in his right hand his graduation certificate for all the world to see. He is beaming!

After the snapshot, Brett gave me a huge bearhug. Then, his hands on my shoulders, he looked me directly in the eyes. "Major Doss," he said, "this is the greatest day in my life. This is the very first time I ever completed anything I started. I thank you and Mrs. Doss so much. Though I certainly know it's all uphill from now on, I promise to work hard to apply all that you have taught me and all that I learned in Narcotics Anonymous. I know that, leaning on my Higher Power, Jesus Christ, I will remain clean and sober."

Following the ceremony, I called the family up to the platform. My hand in Brett's, I led the congregation in prayer for him—that he would continue to grow in Christ and lean on God for guidance and strength, harnessing God's great power to keep him clean and sober, every day, one day at a time.

Two days later, John Wood, my director of retail, pulled me aside and sought my approval to hire Brett to work as a clerk in one of our thrift stores. "Are you sure that's what you want to do?" I asked him.

"Absolutely, Major. Brett's a hard worker and honest. I know he's got a few rough edges; he has to work on his interpersonal skills."

"That's right," I said. "In the course of the program he got in trouble more than once. Interpersonal skills are particularly important in a store setting, where good customer relations are so very crucial."

"I have faith he can do it," John insisted. "And I'll work with him to see he acquires the skills he needs. He has to learn sometime; why not now?"

"Okay," I finally said. "I hope and pray it will work out for him and for us."

The next day, as I was crossing the warehouse lot, Brett spotted me and came running. "Thanks so much for giving me a chance in the stores!" he exclaimed. "It's a great opportunity for me. I know I wasn't the model beneficiary. But I promise I will make you a good employee. You will be glad you gave me this opportunity."

He shook my hand until I thought he might shake it off. I grinned. "It's up to you, Brett. Work hard and pray hard, and you will succeed. John has faith in you. I have faith in you."

And sure enough, Brett succeeded. While there were certainly some occasions when John had to intervene to calm him down and strongly counsel him, Brett continued to improve. John explained to me, "The reason Brett is succeeding is because he wants so very much to do so. He is determined to grow out of his shortcomings. He gets frustrated easily, and this is his failing, but he listens when I counsel him. He hangs on to my every word and, in fact, quotes them back to me periodically. It's like I'm a textbook he is studying."

Then early one morning the jolting call came. I had been up late the night before going over a mountain of paperwork. At 1 a.m., I finally laid it aside. And it seemed I had just rested my head on my pillow when the phone rang. Painfully opening one eye, I noticed that the clock showed 3 a.m. *Who can that be at this hour of the morning?* I wondered. It rang again. Groggily, I reached out and picked up the phone.

"Hello."

"Hello, Major? Major, this is Brett."

I heard my wife turn over. "Who is it?" she asked sleepily.

"It's Brett," I told her. "Brett, what's going on?"

The air was thick with silence. Finally he replied, "Remember, Major, how you said that if I felt an overpowering urge to do drugs again I could call you, no matter what time of the day or night?"

"Yes. That's right. I remember."

"Well, my sister called last night. My mom, she just passed away." His voice broke. "At least she got to see me clean and sober for a little while before...." He became quiet. I heard sniffles on the other end of the line; he was crying. "I treated her so badly for so long! Now I want to go get high just to end this horrible feeling of shame and regret! I'm losing control of the urge—I'm going to give in—I know it! Major, can you come pray with me before I completely lose control, 'cause there's no going back once I give in!"

"I'm so sorry, Brett. Let's pray *now*!" I emphasized. And I prayed intensely over the phone, "Dear Lord, please comfort Brett right now and strengthen him. May he harness your power in a special way as he attempts to come to grips with this tragedy in his life. His mother has passed on. You know that, Lord, and you know just how much Brett is hurting right now. I know you love him dearly and want him to remain clean and sober. Help him keep strong in the face of his overwhelming obsession to do drugs. Please strengthen him, Lord. Strengthen him."

"Yes, Lord. Please, Lord," Brett interjected between sobs.

"Brett, where are you?" I demanded. When he told me, I replied: "I'll meet you at the center in 30 minutes. I'll be there as quick as I can. Can you meet me?" It was agreed.

As I drove, I thought back over the months at how far Brett had progressed since his first arrival in our program. It seemed as if he had passed over from adolescence to adulthood, he had made such tremendous strides. He had over a year of sobriety under his belt now. It was so important that he surmount this hurdle, that he not give in, especially considering all his hard work and the terrific progress he had made.

Driving in the dark, I kept seeing his face, so alive with eagerness to learn as he participated in the worship services and Bible studies. Sometimes he reminded me of a sponge, the way he soaked it all in. He was finally experiencing the joy of the journey when this heavy blow had fallen. His mother, whom he loved so dearly, had suddenly passed away. A strong woman, she had displayed great patience with her son during the difficult years. From the day Brett checked into the facility, he said he wanted to stay clean and sober for her. He owed her so much.

It was still quite dark as I pulled into the parking lot. As I walked up the steps to the lobby, the cat that the men had taken in scurried past me. All else was deathly quiet. The night watchman was sitting at his post, writing notes in a pad. He looked up and waved as I entered.

I spotted Brett immediately. He was sitting in a corner chair facing away from the lobby, so I saw him before he saw me. He looked very scared. His eyes were wet. He was slouched, almost hunched over, the very image of doom and dejection. When he spotted me, he reminded me of a child perking up at the sight of a long-lost parent. The 36-year-old spun to his feet, ran over and wrapped his arms about me, hugging me with all his worth. "Thanks for coming, Major! Thanks for coming! I'm so sorry for calling you so late at night like this."

"I'm sorry, Brett, about your mom," I remarked, returning the embrace.

Taking him by the shoulder, I walked slowly with him into the dimly lit chapel, continuing up to the front where we knelt before the holiness table. Laying a hand upon Brett's shoulder, I prayed aloud for him. And then he prayed. Alternately, we prayed loud and long there in the wee morning hours, calling on the power of God as hard as we could.

Brett's confession to God (as well as to me as I prayed with him) was profound and intimately personal as he bared his heart to his Lord. I was moved and deeply honored that he saw me as a father-figure and a respected confidant, and he trusted me to share this time with him.

A few hours later we had breakfast together in the residence dining room. In an emotional moment, Brett reached out and placed his hand on mine. "Thank you, Major Doss. Thank you," he said, looking me directly in the eyes. That silent look of gratitude spoke volumes.

"Thank God, Brett. Not me. It's his doing. We owe him all the glory."

He nodded. He understood.

Brett surmounted that hurdle with flying colors; he remained clean and sober. A few months later, John Wood promoted Brett to manager of the store where he was working. A year later, when my wife and I received marching orders, Brett was among the many who gathered to wish us bon voyage.

Two years after reporting to our new appointment, I received a phone call out of the blue that knocked my socks off. It was Brett. He was getting married and wanted me to perform the ceremony. So it was that one month later, with my wife Mary at the piano, I stood in the sanctum of a Methodist church and joined Brett and his fiancée, Melanie, in the bonds of holy matrimony. Brett was now managing a store for Goodwill Enterprises, earning much more than he had been with The Salvation Army; yet there was John Wood, my former director of retail, looking on proudly as Brett held the hand of his bride.

And I prayed aloud: "Dear Lord, we thank you for the union of the hearts of Brett and Melanie. We ask you to guard them well as they strike out on this new relationship. We sincerely pray that you bless this couple with a love that will last forever. We pray they remain fully focused on the divine revelation of the purpose of their partnership. In sickness and health, in temptation and inspiration, may they receive your counsel and find your strength. In hurts and failures may they see your light. In desperation and loneliness may they find both your sweet pardon and your joy. But most of all, dear Lord, we pray you may bless them with a family healthy, bright, and strong, filled with faith, hope, and joy and, especially, dear Jesus, that is centered on your love."

BIBLE SELECTION

Praise the Lord.
Praise the Lord, O my soul.
I will praise the Lord all my life;
I will sing praise to my God as long as I live.

Do not put your trust in princes,
in mortal men, who cannot save.
When their spirit departs, they return to the ground;
on that very day their plans come to nothing.

Blessed is he whose help is the God of Jacob,
whose hope is in the Lord his God,
the Maker of heaven and earth,
the sea, and everything in them—
the Lord who remains faithful forever.
He upholds the cause of the oppressed

and gives food to the hungry.
The Lord sets prisoners free,
the Lord gives sight to the blind,
the Lord lifts up those who are bowed down,
the Lord loves the righteous.
The Lord watches over the alien
and sustains the fatherless and the widow,
but he frustrates the ways of the wicked.

The Lord reigns forever,
your God, O Zion, for all generations.

Praise the Lord (Ps. 146 NIV).

REFLECTION

What a joy to watch this angry, coarse, unchurched young man transform into a grateful, thoughtful, caring person. I was fortunate to be there when he gave his heart to the Lord. He beat the odds, it seemed to me. So many we lose, so many relapse, so many die, but Brett survived. He was determined to remain clean and sober, and he succeeded. What a joy and a privilege to witness this transformational experience!

And how delightful to see him three years later with his bride!

Brett's victory over his drug addiction was by no means a simple thing, and he would be the first to say that it was not his doing but God's. It was a victory over *the powers of this dark world and against the spiritual forces of evil in the heavenly realms* (Eph. 6:12 NIV), and this was something only God could bring about. God did it, and I was ever so humbly thankful that I could be useful to God, to serve as an instrument in his hands. Thank you, Lord, so very much. Thank you for the honor of serving you.

In the precious name of Jesus Christ my Savior I pray. Amen.

CHAPTER TWENTY-SEVEN

Further Reflections On the Journey

And we all, who with unveiled faces contemplate the Lord's glory,
are being transformed into his image with ever-increasing glory,
which comes from the Lord, who is the Spirit (2 Cor. 3:18 TNIV).

GOD HAS RADICALLY TRANSFORMED Brett and hundreds of others in our Salvation Army programs. Since I turned my life and will over to him 20 years ago, God has also radically transformed me—from a hostile, self-destructive individual to one who can finally serve as an instrument of his will. God took an angry, selfish man, full of resentments—a greatly soiled, deformed creature—and shaped him into an empathetic, caring person. Such a dramatic transformation, however, is never instantaneous. My journey continues to be one of a gradual metamorphosis.

You see, before I can completely let go of who I used to be, I must continue to attentively progress through the realm of experience, bit by bit, recognizing old, mistaken ways of thinking for what they are, and replacing them with new and better ways (God's ways) of doing things. This is true of every human being. The apostle Paul provides us with directions:

> *So here's what I want you to do, God helping you:* **Take your**
> **everyday, ordinary life—your sleeping, eating, going-to-**
> **work, and walking-around life—and place it before God as**
> **an offering.**... *Don't become so well-adjusted to your culture that*
> *you fit into it without even thinking. Instead,* **fix your attention**
> **on God.** *You'll be changed from the inside out.* **Readily recognize**
> **what he wants from you, and quickly respond to it.** *Unlike*
> *the culture around you, always dragging you down to its level of*
> *immaturity, God brings the best out of you, develops well-formed*
> *maturity in you* (Rom. 12:1-2 MSG, emphasis mine).

This is an excellent prescription for the transformation of our thinking and the behavior that should follow once we present ourselves to God as a love-offering. The more complete the surrender of ourselves, the more operative his power within us, for as Paul proclaims, God is *able to do immeasurably more than all we ask or imagine,* **according to his power that is at work within us** (Eph. 3:20-21 NIV, emphasis mine). The esteemed 20th century writer on mysticism, Evelyn Underhill, explains: "Were we more sensitive to the delicate forces that enmesh and penetrate us, we should feel the operation of that Spirit within all circumstances; increasing in power and clearness with the degree of surrender achieved by those who are its instruments."[17]

Since God is omnipotent, his considerable help empowers the surrendered person to deal more effectively with life's innumerable challenges and hurdles: *But we have this treasure in jars of clay to show that this all-surpassing power is from God and not from us. We are hard pressed on every side, but not crushed; perplexed, but not in despair; persecuted, but not abandoned; struck down, but not destroyed* (2 Cor. 4:7-9 NIV).

However, effecting the self-surrender essential to tap into God's immense reservoir of strength is by no means as straightforward as it may appear. Many well-intentioned people fall far short, I believe, because *merely making the mental decision* to give up our self-control and hand the reins of our lives over to God is never enough. All our natural instincts rebel against such a yielding; our mere mortal identity adheres to us more stubbornly than glue. Such dependence upon ourselves to run our own lives is a deeply entrenched habit which only God can put down (Matt. 19:26). Hence David's prayer: *Search me, oh God, and know my heart; test me and know my anxious thoughts. Point out anything in me that offends you, and lead me along the path of everlasting life* (Ps. 139:23-24 NLT).

Thomas Merton describes an essential ingredient in this self-transformation process:

> Our destiny is to live out what we think, because unless we live what we know, we do not even know it.... *Living is the constant adjustment of thought to life and life to thought in such a way that we are always growing.... Real self-conquest is the conquest of ourselves not by ourselves but by the Holy Spirit....* Yet before we can surrender ourselves we must become ourselves. For no one can give up what he does not possess.[18] (emphasis mine)

Merton's observations are quite profound and very accurate. That which we think at a subliminal level—in the part of our minds that defines who we really are, yet remains largely inaccessible to us—is revealed to us by God *only as we live it out in our self-surrendered life.* This is a region into which only God can shed light. And to do this, to plunge head on into this unconscious terrain, is absolutely essential if we are to progress spiritually. Yet it is by no means pain-free. It hurts.

For all believers, spiritual progress is contingent upon three interdependent and systemic behaviors. We encountered them in our reading of Romans 12:1-2 (as presented in The Message):

1. Take your everyday, ordinary life ... and place it before God as an offering;
2. Fix your attention on God; and
3. Readily recognize what he wants from you, and quickly respond to it.

Merton describes this process in the following passage:

> To work out our own identity in God, which the Bible calls "working out our salvation" [Phil. 2:12], is a labor that requires sacrifice and anguish, risk and many tears. It demands close attention to reality at every moment, and great fidelity to God as He reveals Himself, obscurely, in the mystery of each situation. We do not know clearly beforehand what the result of this work will be. The secret of my full identity is hidden in Him. He alone can make me who I am, or rather who I will be when at last I fully begin to be.[19]

Remaining attentive to divine guidance, harnessing God's power in one's life, one can explore the subliminal reaches of his own mind and discover the hidden truths which must be found—and perhaps purged—if he is to find his true identity in God. Merton also reminds us that the journey is often painful, that spiritual growth "requires sacrifice and anguish, risk and many tears." That old saint of The Salvation Army, Commissioner Samuel Logan Brengle, would certainly agree. He writes:

Spiritual leadership is not won nor established by promotion, but by many prayers and tears. It is attained by confessions of sin, and much heart-searching and humbling before God; by self-surrender, a courageous sacrifice of every idol, a bold, deathless, uncompromising, and uncomplaining embrace of the Cross, and by an eternal, unfaltering looking unto Jesus crucified.[20]

Over the years following my spiritual conversion, more than once I pulled myself up short with the abrupt realization that I was thinking and behaving in the old manner—excluding God. Since insightful self-revelation can be very painful, we instinctively tend to steer clear of it. And because of this hesitation to look honestly at myself, my old behavior patterns continued to rule the day. But I finally came to see that the full reality of who I am lies deeply hidden within my unconscious self; however, I cannot make an intentional decision to change that of which I am ignorant. Bottom line: I had to consciously reason that I love God enough to permit him to reveal to me who I truly am—no matter how painful the experience.

The fact that we are unaware of our biases is the very reason they rule us; they remain hidden within the deepest recesses of our being. Remember the old adage: "Fish discover water last"? That which is nearest to us, as close to us as our own skin, we do not see, because it is part and parcel of the lens through which we view the world. Just as we require assistance to look at the backs of our own heads, so we need help to peer within ourselves and examine what lies there. And it is crucial that we do so.

If we humbly and sincerely ask him, God will help us; we can harness his immense power within our own lives. Then, as we "live out what we think," remaining prayerfully attentive and introspective, God will empower us to see ourselves as we really are as compared to the person he wishes us to become. It is absolutely necessary that we permit him to do this and then allow him to excavate the very core of beings, ridding us of the self-destructive content—and this requires a willingness to suffer for his sake.

A. W. Tozer presents a very clear picture of this:

Self is the opaque veil that hides the face of God from us [2 Cor. 3:14-18]. *It can be removed only in spiritual experience, never by mere instruction.*

We may as well try to instruct leprosy out of our system.... *We must prepare ourselves for an ordeal of suffering* in some measure like that through which our Savior passed when he suffered under Pontius Pilate.... In human experience that veil is made of living tissue; it is composed of the sentient, quivering stuff of which our whole being consists, and *to touch it is to touch us where we feel pain. To tear it away is to injure us, to hurt us and make us bleed.... To rip through the dear and tender stuff of which life is made can never be anything but deeply painful.* Yet that is what the cross did to Jesus and it is what the cross would do to every man to set him free.[21] (emphasis mine)

It hurt a great deal when in midlife I finally acknowledged my cold-hearted arrogance in adopting an atheistic mindset. It was also exceedingly painful to confront the bigotry which, unbeknownst to me, had ruled me for so long. To accept my selfishness and egoism for what it was—and to admit how much it hurt my loved ones—was very disconcerting, yet nevertheless absolutely necessary! Taking off the blinders, painfully acknowledging the truth, is critical to God turning us around. Such spiritual growth is by its very nature gradual as we move in the direction that God points us.

In John's gospel we find this teaching by Christ himself (rendered here in the words of Eugene Peterson):

Then Jesus turned to the Jews who had claimed to believe in him. **"If you stick with this, living out what I tell you, you are my disciples for sure. Then you will experience for yourselves the truth, and the truth will free you**.... *I tell you most solemnly that anyone who chooses a life of sin is trapped in a dead-end life and is, in fact, a slave....* **So if the Son sets you free, you are free through and through"** (John 8:31-32, 34, 36 MSG, emphasis mine).

Jesus points out that if we "stick with" his teaching, "living [it] out" in our daily lives, we will "experience" for ourselves his person, since it is he who is *"the way and the* **truth** *and the life"* (John 14:6 NIV, emphasis mine). Consequently, we will come to know him better and better (2 Pe. 3:18). This growing intimacy with Christ—our increasing personal experience of the grand reality of who he is—will free us from the enslavement of sin (John 8:34; Rom. 6:16), that bondage of self-centeredness into which we are all born (Matt. 16:24; Ps. 51:5).

Christ reminds us that if we prayerfully, attentively live our lives in the light of his own (John 8:12), he will show us *as we live them out* those aspects of our thinking and behavior that need to be brought into conformance with his will. *"Take my yoke upon you and learn from me,"* he entreats us (Matt. 11:29 NIV), imploring us to willfully become his students along the pathways of life, himself yoked alongside us, bearing the brunt of the burden, as he teaches us a better way, his way (John 14:26). We *"experience for [ourselves] the truth [of Christ],"* and his power subsequently frees us from enslavement to selfishness (John 8:32). We learn as we go. It is a process.

This is the journey upon which I embarked in 1986 after accepting Christ as my Savior just a few months shy of my 40th birthday. God brought me along this journey full of many errors and regrets, as well as victories and joy. The course took me from a mindset of hostility to one of hospitality—from a self-centered, self-destructive misanthrope to one who strives to be of service to others, loving God and all people. *Nothing [is] between us and God, our faces shining with the brightness of his face. And so we are transfigured much like the Messiah, our lives gradually becoming brighter and more beautiful as God enters our lives and we become like him* (2 Cor. 3:18 MSG).

Thank you, Lord, for your exorbitant patience with me. Thank you for bringing me so far. There has been much sacrifice and anguish, risk, and many regrets, yet the journey has most certainly been worth it all. You changed me from a man who had given up on life into one of patience and much love. Now no matter what blows the world may yet hold in store for me, I have your peace locked within my heart, along with my love for you and all humanity. And I know a heavenly home awaits. Therefore I push on, striving unceasingly to be a more and more effective witness of you in my life. I exist but to love and serve you.

In the precious name of Jesus Christ my Savior I pray. Amen.

NOTES

1. Rufus Jones, *Rufus Jones: Essential Writings* (Maryknoll, NY: Orbis Books, 2001), 80.
2. Ernest Becker, *The Denial of Death* (New York: The Free Press, 1973), ix.
3. Dallas Willard, *Renovation of the Heart* (Colorado Springs: NavPress, 2002), 52.
4. E. Stanley Jones, *Abundant Living* (Nashville: Abingdon, 1942), 7.
5. Bertrand Russell, *Why I Am Not a Christian and other essays on religion and related subjects* (New York: Simon & Schuster, Inc., 1957), 6-7.
6. Jones, *Abundant Living,* 43.
7. Willard, *Renovation of the Heart,* 51.
8. Soren Kierkegaard, *The Sickness Unto Death* (London: Penguin Books, 1989), 158.
9. *Alcoholics Anonymous* (New York: Alcoholics Anonymous World Services, Inc., 1976), 46.
10. Thomas Kelly, *The Eternal Promise: A Sequel to a Testament of Devotion* (Richmond, IN: Friends United Press, 1988), 38.
11. Ibid., 39.
12. Ravi Zacharias, *Can Man Live Without God* (Nashville: W. Publishing Group, 1994), 53.
13. Jones, *Abundant Living,* 12.
14. T.S. Elliot, *T.S. Eliot: Collected Poems 1909-1962* (New York: Harcourt Brace & Company, 1991), "Little Gidding," stanza 5, 208.
15. Soren Kierkegaard, *Fear and Trembling* (New York: Penguin Books, 1985), 75.
16. Ibid., 73.
17. Evelyn Underhill, *The Golden Sequence: A Fourfold Study of the Spiritual Life* (Eugene, OR: Wipf and Stock Publishers, 2003), 71.
18. Thomas Merton, *Thoughts in Solitude* (Boston, MA: Shambhala Publications, Inc., 1986), 16-18.
19. Thomas Merton, *New Seeds of Contemplation* (New York: New Directions Publishing Company, 1972), 32-33.
20. Samuel Logan Brengle, *The Soul-Winner's Secret* (Atlanta: The Salvation Army Supplies and Purchasing Department, 1976), 22-23.
21. A.W. Tozer, *The Pursuit of God* (Camp Hill, PA: Christian Publications, 1983), 43.

BIBLIOGRAPHY

Alcoholics Anonymous. New York: Alcoholics Anonymous World Services, Inc., 1976.

Becker, Ernest. *The Denial of Death*. New York: The Free Press, 1973.

Brengle, Samuel Logan. *The Soul-Winner's Secret*. Atlanta: The Salvation Army Supplies and Purchasing Department, 1976.

Elliot, T.S. *T.S. Eliot: Collected Poems 1909-1962*. New York: Harcourt Brace & Company, 1991.

Jones, E. Stanley. *Abundant Living*. Nashville: Abingdon, 1942.

Jones, Rufus. *Rufus Jones: Essential Writings*. Maryknoll, NY: Orbis Books, 2001.

Kelly, Thomas. *The Eternal Promise: A Sequel to a Testament of Devotion*. Richmond, IN: Friends United Press, 1988.

Kierkegaard, Soren. *Fear and Trembling*. New York: Penguin Books, 1985.

Kierkegaard, Soren. *The Sickness Unto Death*. London: Penguin Books, 1989.

Merton, Thomas. *New Seeds of Contemplation*. New York: New Directions Publishing Company, 1972.

Merton, Thomas. *Thoughts in Solitude*. Boston: Shambhala Publications, Inc., 1986.

Russell, Bertrand. *Why I Am Not a Christian and other essays on religion and related subjects*. New York: Simon & Schuster, Inc., 1957.

Tozer, A.W. *The Pursuit of God*. Camp Hill, PA: Christian Publications, 1983.

Underhill, Evelyn. *The Golden Sequence: A Fourfold Study of the Spiritual Life*. Eugene, OR: Wipf and Stock Publishers, 2003.

Willard, Dallas. *Renovation of the Heart*. Colorado Springs: NavPress, 2002.

Zacharias, Ravi. *Can Man Live Without God*. Nashville: W. Publishing